MACHIAVELLI

Eminent Lives, a series of brief biographies by distinguished authors on canonical figures, joins a long tradition in this lively form, from Plutarch's *Lives* to Vasari's *Lives of the Painters*, Dr. Johnson's *Lives of the Poets* to Lytton Strachey's *Eminent Victorians*. Pairing great subjects with writers known for their strong sensibilities and sharp, lively points of view, the Eminent Lives are ideal introductions designed to appeal to the general reader, the student, and the scholar. "To preserve a becoming brevity which excludes everything that is redundant and nothing that is significant," wrote Strachey: "That, surely, is the first duty of the biographer."

GENERAL EDITOR: JAMES ATLAS

ALSO BY ROSS KING

Michelangelo and the Pope's Ceiling

*The Judgment of Paris: The Revolutionary Decade
That Gave the World Impressionism*

*Brunelleschi's Dome: How a Renaissance
Genius Reinvented Architecture*

Ex-Libris

Domino

MACHIAVELLI

Philosopher of Power

Ross King

EMINENT LIVES

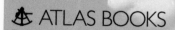 ATLAS BOOKS

 HarperCollins*Publishers*

HarperCollins books may be purchased for educational, business, or sales promotional use. For information, please write: Special Markets Department, HarperCollins Publishers, 10 East 53rd Street, New York, NY 10022.

FIRST EDITION

Designed by Elliott Beard

Maps courtesy of Reginald Piggott

Library of Congress Cataloging-in-Publication Data is available upon request.

ISBN-13: 978-0-06-081717-6
ISBN-10: 0-06-081717-8

07 08 09 10 11   ID/RRD   10 9 8 7 6 5 4 3 2 1

For Christopher Sinclair-Stevenson

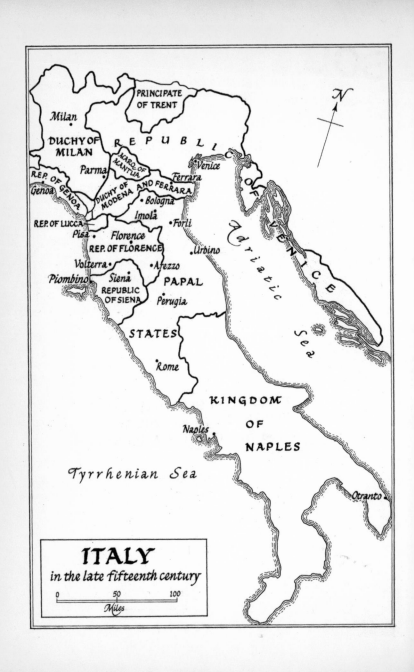

ITALY
in the late fifteenth century

0   50   100
Miles

MACHIAVELLI

Chapter One

A STRANGE NEW type of insect appeared in the meadows beside the river Arno in Florence in the summer of 1498. These swarms of gold-bodied caterpillars had a human face—eyes and a nose could be distinguished—while on the head was a golden halo and a small cross. They quickly became known as "Brother Girolamo's caterpillars."

"Brother Girolamo" was Girolamo Savonarola, a charismatic, green-eyed Dominican friar from Ferrara who for the previous six years had dominated Florence's spiritual and political life with his fire-and-brimstone sermons. By 1498, however, his mesmeric hold over the city had finally been broken. He was excommunicated by Pope Alexander VI in the summer of 1497, and less than a year later, on the morning of May 23, 1498, he was hanged in the city's main piazza as punishment for, in the words of one chronicler, "stirring up discord in Florence and of disseminating doctrine that was not entirely Catholic."[1] Cut down from the scaffold, his body was consumed on a bonfire; afterward his ashes were thrown into the Arno from the Ponte Vecchio, washing downstream to the spot where, a few weeks later, the caterpillars mysteriously appeared.

Savonarola was not the only casualty in Florence in May of 1498. Two Dominican priests were hanged beside him, while other supporters of Savonarola—known by their opponents as *Piagnoni* (Snivelers)—suffered equally unpleasant fates. The friar's most powerful political ally, Francesco Valori, was murdered with a billhook; a bolt from a crossbow killed Valori's wife. Dozens of other *Piagnoni* were fined or deprived of their political rights, and several friars from the convent of San Marco, where Savonarola had served as prior, were sent into exile. Even the bell of San Marco, nicknamed *La Piagnona*, did not escape punishment: it was removed from its tower and given a public flogging before it, too, was exiled from Florence.

Retribution reached the highest levels of government as the Signoria—Florence's ruling council—began an immediate purge of Savonarola's sympathizers from their official posts. All ten members of the *Dieci di Libertà e Pace* ("Ten of Liberty and Peace"), who handled foreign policy, were dismissed, as were the eight men comprising the *Otto di Guardia* ("Eight of the Watch"), the committee in charge of criminal justice. Also losing his post was an official in the Chancellery named Alessandro Braccesi. His replacement was a twenty-nine-year-old political novice named Niccolò Machiavelli. Twenty-nine— the age of eligibility for voting—was a remarkably young age for a man to hold such an important post. Most young men in

Florence remained under the authority of their fathers until the age of twenty-four, and some did not achieve their legal majority until twenty-eight. But Machiavelli would make up for his youth and inexperience with a formidable intellect and an impeccable education, and with tremendous amounts of energy and ambition.

Machiavelli had been born in Florence on May 3, 1469, the eldest son of Bernardo Machiavelli and his wife, Bartolomea. "I was born in poverty," Niccolò would later write, "and at an early age learned how to scrimp rather than to thrive."[2] Like many things he wrote, this claim is something of an overstatement. His mother seems to have descended from an ancient and distinguished family, while his father came from a prosperous clan that for many generations had owned large tracts of land in the rolling, vine-clad hills south of Florence. It is true that Bernardo Machiavelli was by no means a rich man. He once described himself on a tax document, all too truthfully, as being "without gainful employment."[3] But he lived in a large house in the Santo Spirito quarter of Florence, near the Ponte Vecchio, and he also owned a farm outside Florence in the village of Sant' Andrea in Percussina, complete with vineyards, apple orchards, olive trees, and livestock. His rural possessions furthermore included a tavern and a butcher shop.

Bernardo Machiavelli had trained for a legal career and then pursued, not very diligently or successfully, a career as a notary. However, he evidently enjoyed a reputation in Florence as a first-class legal brain. He became friends with the chancellor of Florence, an eminent scholar named Bartolomeo Scala, who featured him as a legal expert in a 1483 treatise entitled *Dialogue on Laws and Legal Judgments*. But Bernardo's most notable trait was his passion for books. His formal education would have seen him studying Latin grammar, perfecting his handwriting, and learning how to compose wills and certify business and marriage contracts. His mind roved more broadly and searchingly over human affairs than such paperwork would suggest, and by the 1470s he was dabbling in classical literature. Scala's *Dialogue* may well have done him justice by having him knowledgeably quote authors such as Plato, Justinian, Cicero, and Lactantius. Bernardo certainly acquired for his personal library, sometimes at no mean expense, editions of works by writers such as Livy and Macrobius; and he borrowed books, when he could not afford to buy them, from institutions such as the library of the convent of Santa Croce. One of his most prized possessions was an edition of Livy's *History of Rome* that he acquired for free by compiling an index of place names for its Florentine printer. Eleven years later, in 1486, he had the volume bound in leather, a task for which he compensated the binder with three bottles of red wine from his estate in the country.

Bernardo was far from alone in his reverence for classical literature and history. An intense preoccupation with the culture of the ancient world had placed Florence at the forefront of new intellectual and artistic activities—what later came to be known as "humanism"—that shifted the intellectual emphasis from theology to the more secular studies that had once been the bedrock of classical literature. The head of the Florentine

Chancellery between 1375 and 1406, a scholar named Coluccio Salutati, had argued that classical texts could teach important lessons about contemporary moral and political life not found in the Bible. He and his followers approached the texts of the ancients in a hands-on fashion, treating them, in effect, as how-to manuals replete with practical wisdom about everyday civil and moral life. They believed the works of the ancient Greeks and Romans could demonstrate, among other things, how best to educate children, deliver a speech, become a good citizen, or govern a state—actions and pursuits that would make a person (and a society) happy and prosperous.

The humanists offered fifteenth-century Europeans a new way of looking at the world, and at man's place in it. They took their inspiration from, among other sources, the claim by the Greek philosopher Protagoras that "man is the measure of all things." For medieval Christians, the government, laws, and morals of a society were fixed by God, but for the humanists of the fifteenth century, as for the ancient Greeks and Romans, these institutions were man-made and, as such, both worthy of scrutiny and susceptible to change. Though many human-ists were devout Christians, their interest lay in human affairs rather than transcendental values. Critically, they emphasized the classical rather than the Christian view of human nature: man was seen not as corrupted by original sin and in need of salvation through God's grace but as free, creative, and self-determining, capable of both higher reason and base passions.

Bernardo seems to have been determined that, despite the costs involved, his son should receive the benefits of the humanist culture flourishing in Florence. Three days after his seventh birthday, Niccolò began learning the elements of Latin under the supervision of a local teacher known as Maestro Matteo, who conducted lessons from a house near the Ponte Santa Trinità, a short distance from the Machiavelli home. Within a few years he was studying arithmetic and composing in Latin under the tutelage of a more distinguished master by the name of Paolo da Ronciglione. A teacher of some reputation, Paolo was also a friend and colleague of the great humanist scholar Cristoforo Landino, whose commentary on Dante, published in 1481, so impressed Florence's city fathers that—such was the esteem in which poets and scholars were held in those days— he was rewarded with a castle.

Machiavelli then seems to have progressed to the institution in which Landino himself held his professorship in poetry and oratory, the Studio Fiorentino, a university founded in 1348 but relocated in 1473 to Pisa. Virtually nothing is known of Machiavelli's school days, but it seems safe to assume that he prospered in the lively intellectual atmosphere of the Studio. He was an enchanting companion. He might have been an unprepossessing physical specimen, slenderly built as he was, with thin lips, a weak chin, sunken cheeks, and closely cropped black hair. But he had a sharp wit and a love of jollity and farce that belied the ascetic appearance; most portraits of him—albeit made posthumously—would feature an ironic smile playing at his lips. Though a voracious reader of the classics, he could also devote himself to less elevated pursuits, such as gambling and the company of prostitutes. According to one friend, he "abounded in charm and drolleries," while another claimed his jokes and witticisms made everyone "split their sides laughing." He became known as "Machia," a pun on *macchia*, meaning a smear or a stain: a reference to the damage inflicted by his sharp tongue and irreverent wit.

The Studio would have given Machiavelli a solid grounding in such core disciplines of the humanist syllabus as rhetoric, grammar, poetry, history, and moral philosophy. One text he appears to have studied with some care, since he copied out the 7,400-line poem by hand, was the Roman philosopher Lucretius's *De rerum natura* (On the Nature of Things), the sole manuscript of which had been rediscovered and brought back to Florence in 1417. The young Machiavelli may well have been intrigued by the central argument of Lucretius: that fear and religious superstition should be banished by means of the application of reason and a close study of the inner workings of nature.[4]

Machiavelli concerned himself with poetry as well as philosophy. Three of his youthful efforts were collected together in a volume of poetry illustrated with drawings by the painter Sandro Botticelli. The volume also included ten poems by Lorenzo de' Medici (called "the Magnificent"), who had been the de facto ruler of Florence from 1469—the year, coincidentally, of Machiavelli's birth—until his death in 1492. The Medici were the wealthiest and most powerful family in Florence. Lorenzo's grandfather, Cosimo de' Medici, son of the richest banker in Europe, had become the virtual overlord of Florence in 1434 after ousting the existing government. The family had then maintained control of the city for six decades, nominally respecting the republic's institutions but in fact concentrating power in the hands of their supporters.

Cosimo and Lorenzo had both been generous and discerning patrons of the arts, funded churches and palaces, and provided support for the famous Neoplatonic Academy that met outside Florence at the Villa di Careggi. Just how close Machiavelli was to the Medici remains a matter of conjecture. He seems to have been, at least for a time, a member of the circle of humanist scholars, artists, and philosophers (an exalted group that included the young Michelangelo) who were cultivated by Lorenzo. One of Machiavelli's poems was even dedicated to Giuliano de' Medici, Lorenzo's youngest son, who would have been an adolescent when the poems were collected in the early 1490s. Whatever the nature of the association, it was dramatically severed in 1494, when a popular uprising against Lorenzo's arrogant and incompetent eldest son Piero (known as *Lo Sfortunato*, "the Unfortunate") forced the Medici into exile.

By the time he reached his late twenties, Machiavelli had found the career in which to exploit his many talents. Politics was in the Machiavelli blood. Over the previous two centuries, numerous members of the clan had held political office in Florence. Altogether, thirteen Machiavelli had at one time or another been elevated to the highest civic post, that of Gonfalonier (Standard-bearer) of Justice. The most colorful career had been that forged by Giovanni Machiavelli, a contemporary of Dante who was elected to high office on several occasions despite having murdered a priest and been accused of rape.

The only other Machiavelli to make names for themselves were Francesco and Girolamo, second cousins of Bernardo: both were beheaded for opposing Cosimo de' Medici's oligarchic regime.

Undaunted by the fate of these relations, Niccolò seems to have plunged into politics in the tempestuous months preceding Savonarola's downfall. Early in 1498 he contested the post of First Secretary of the Signoria, an office that offered administrative support to the republic's ruling council. Running against three other candidates, he failed to garner enough votes, possibly due to his anti-Savonarolian credentials.[5] But the winds of change blew him into office soon enough. Three months later, hard on the heels of Savonarola's death and the aggressive persecution of the *Piagnoni*, he enjoyed a happier result. On May 28, 1498, the Council of Eighty, the board in charge of appointing the republic's ambassadors and other officials, nominated him for the important and prestigious post of Second Chancellor. As the appointment required ratification, his name was sent before an assembly of some 3,000 citizens known as the Great Council of the People. Machiavelli once again found himself with three rivals for the post, but this time, on June 19, he was elected to serve what remained of Alessandro Braccesi's two-year term. The man whose name would later become synonymous with ruthless, ironfisted rule came to power on the strength of ballots cast by his fellow citizens.

Florence, a city with some 50,000 people inside its ring of walls, had reconstituted itself as a republic following the expulsion of the Medici in 1494. The Great Council of the People was the republic's cornerstone, an assembly of Florentine men over the age of twenty-nine who had the right to vote on legislation and elect officers proposed to them by the Signoria, the executive arm of government. The Signoria was constituted by eight Signori (or Lords) and the official head of the government, the Gonfalonier of Justice. These nine men formed the republic's policy in consultation with various committees, such as the Ten of Liberty and Peace and the Eight of the Watch. All of their correspondence—reports, letters, treaties—was prepared by the secretaries in the Chancellery.

The Florentine Chancellery was no ordinary bureaucracy. For more than a century it had been staffed by some of the most brilliant literary minds in Florence: poets, historians, scholars of Latin and Greek. The government's official correspondence, always conducted in Latin, was, accordingly, of the highest literary standard, Coluccio Salutati having initiated the practice of peppering official documents with classical quotations and allusions. This tradition of literary excellence was ably maintained by the man elected First Chancellor in 1498, Marcello Virgilio Adriani, a scholar of Greek who, in addition to his role in the Chancellery, served as professor of poetry and rhetoric at the Studio Fiorentino. Alessandro Braccesi had been equally accomplished, composing three volumes of poetry in Latin and translating into Italian Aeneas Silvius Piccolomini's *Historia de duobus amantibus*, or "Tale of Two Lovers," a story of adulterous passion written in the 1440s by the man who later became Pope Pius II.

By 1498 as many as fifteen or twenty secretaries, most trained as either notaries or humanist scholars, worked in the Chancellery. Half would be under the supervision of the First Chancellor, who tended to foreign affairs. The others were to serve the Second Chancellor, a position created in 1437 to help deal with the government's increasingly voluminous correspondence. As Second Chancellor, Niccolò Machiavelli would concern himself, at least in theory, with domestic issues. However, the Chancellors were often used by the budget-conscious Signoria as envoys themselves, dispatched to foreign parts with some of the authority, but none of the pomp and expense, of an actual embassy. Furthermore, the Second Chancellor gave administrative support to the Ten of Liberty and Peace, the board overseeing the republic's foreign relations. And in fact on July 14, within a month of entering the Chancellery, Machiavelli was officially appointed Secretary to the Ten, a position ensuring that rather than remaining deskbound in his office, composing reports on domestic affairs, he would be obliged to climb into the saddle and travel abroad with Florentine envoys and ambassadors. Niccolò was about to see the world.

Machiavelli's salary as Second Chancellor was 128 florins, a comfortable though far from luxurious sum given that the average annual earnings of a skilled craftsman in Florence amounted to roughly eighty or ninety florins. He had a number of assistants working under him. Included among them were a friend, Biagio Buonaccorsi, and a notary named Agostino Vespucci, a cousin of the explorer Amerigo Vespucci. All of these functionaries occupied a cramped office in a north-facing room on the second floor of the Palazzo della Signoria, the massive fortress-like construction that served as Florence's seat of government.* This office was reached through a much grander room, the Sala dei Gigli (Hall of the Lilies), that served as the dining room for the Signori. The Hall of the Lilies featured ornate decorations, including a marble doorway and a gilded ceiling. Donatello's marble statue of David presided over the room, and the walls featured frescoes of saints by Michelangelo's first master, Domenico Ghirlandaio.

There was also one further piece of decoration in the Hall of the Lilies. Around about 1400 a Wheel of Fortune had been frescoed above one of its doors, accompanied by a sonnet that warned against placing one's trust in the fickle and capricious goddess Fortuna.[6] This warning must have seemed particularly apt in the days following the dramatic overthrow of Savonarola and his supporters. Fortune, though, seemed to be smiling on Niccolò Machiavelli as, in the summer of 1498, he prepared to take his first steps along the corridors of power.

---

* In the interests of greater historical accuracy, I refer to this building— now known as the Palazzo Vecchio—as the Palazzo della Signoria, its name during Machiavelli's period in office. It did not receive its present name, the "old palace," until the Palazzo Pitti was acquired by the Medici in 1549, at which point the family abandoned the Piazza della Signoria (which they had previously used as their court) for their "new palace" on the south side of the Arno.

Chapter Two

WHEN DOMENICO GHIRLANDAIO completed his fresco cycle of the life of Saint John the Baptist in the church of Santa Maria Novella in Florence, he signed it with a flourish: "In the year 1490, during which this most beautiful city, famous for its victories, arts, and buildings, enjoyed great prosperity, health, and peace." This prosperity, health, and peace was not to last. The years between the death of Lorenzo the Magnificent, in 1492, and that of Girolamo Savonarola, in 1498, had been turbulent and calamitous. A series of bad harvests, caused in part by violent windstorms, had led to famine, and by the spring of 1497 the poor were starving in the streets of Florence. That summer an eclipse of the sun was attended by deaths from plague and fever at a rate of more than a hundred a day. The plague had made regular visits to Florence for a century and a half, most recently in the month of Savonarola's death. To make matters worse, a new disease known as *il male francese*, or "the French disease"—that is, syphilis—had made its appearance, disfiguring its sufferers with boils and in some cases blinding them. It was, according to one Florentine resident, Francesco Guicciardini, "so horrible that it deserves to be mentioned as one of the gravest calamities." Still, in the opinion of many people the greatest catastrophe to befall Florence in those years—indeed, to befall the whole of Italy—had been the invasion of the peninsula by the French under King Charles VIII.

The Italian peninsula in the 1490s was a hodgepodge of more than a dozen independent kingdoms, dukedoms, fiefdoms, city-states, and republics. There were, however, five predominant powers. The two major players in the north were the Duchy of Milan, controlled by the Sforza family, and the Venetian Republic, whose territories and influence extended far inland from its canals and lagoons. The Kingdom of Naples, ruled for the previous fifty years by members of the royal family of Aragón, occupied the southern third of Italy, while much of the central region was taken up by the Papal States, a 250-mile-long tract of land governed by the pope and stretching diagonally across the peninsula from Rome in the south to Bologna in the north. The fifth principal power, Florence, encompassed more than 3,500 square miles of the Tuscan countryside and included the city of Pisa.

These five major powers had more or less been at peace with one another since 1454, when a nonaggression pact, the Peace of Lodi, was agreed to by their representatives. However, the balance had been dramatically upset by the death in

1494 of King Ferdinand I of Naples, known as Don Ferrante. The ambitious young King of France promptly took actions that belied his nickname, Charles the Affable. As the great-grandson of Louis II of Anjou, who had been crowned King of Naples in 1389, Charles VIII possessed a tenuous claim to the Neapolitan kingdom, which the unscrupulous new Duke of Milan, Ludovico Sforza, urged him to press. The result was that in September 1494 the French king, crossing the Alps with an army of more than 30,000 men, forced all of the Italian powers to affirm whether they supported his claim or that of the son of Don Ferrante, the newly crowned King Alfonso II.

The Florentines had given their support at first to Alfonso. However, the appearance on Tuscan soil of the formidable French army, which easily (and brutally) captured the Florentine stronghold of Fivizzano, precipitated a swift change of allegiance, at least in Piero the Unfortunate. Lorenzo the Magnificent had once predicted that his eldest son would cause the fall of the house of Medici through his recklessness and arrogance. This prediction quickly fulfilled itself as, without bothering to consult either the Signoria or the people, the panicked Piero hastily offered Charles his support, along with several Florentine strongholds, including the fortress of Pisa. Such a cowardly surrender outraged the people of Florence, and within days Piero and the rest of his family were fleeing into exile to the shouts of "People and Liberty!" The Florentine people had won their liberty, but what they had lost was almost as valuable: the city of Pisa.

This loss had been, for the Florentines, the most humiliating consequence of the French invasion. Florence had ruled its neighbor, a wealthy port city, since 1406. In November 1494, Charles VIII had signed a treaty with the Florentines promising to return Pisa into their possession as soon as he captured Naples, but the restitution was proving difficult because, as one historian of the day observed, the Pisans were "most inimical by nature against Florentine control." What followed were several years of skirmishes in which the Florentines attempted, unsuccessfully, to retake this valuable possession. In May 1498 the Pisans had trounced the Florentines at San Regolo and—piling on the indignities—captured their military captain, Ludovico da Marciano.

Retaking Pisa was one of the most prominent items on the agenda of the Signoria and the Ten when Niccolò Machiavelli entered the Chancellery in 1498. The problem was made all the more acute by the fact that Florence did not have an army of its own and so, like many other Italian states, was forced to pay others—soldiers of fortune from smaller and poorer Italian states—to fight its battles. For mercantile cities such as Florence, whose citizens devoted themselves to commerce rather than war, these mercenaries, known as *condottieri*, were a necessary evil. One of the main problems was that men who fought for bags of ducats rather than from love of country could not always be expected to perform valiantly on behalf of their employers. The idle, evasive, and duplicitous conduct of the *condottieri* was legendary.

With the hapless Ludovico da Marciano languishing in a Pisan dungeon, the Florentines needed someone else to direct their military assault. In June 1498 they appointed as their new military captain a renowned *condottiere* named Paolo Vitelli, the son of an infamously cruel warlord from the Umbrian town of Città di Castello. Though only thirty-seven, Vitelli had soldiered all over Italy since getting his first taste of action at the age of thirteen. Like many *condottieri*, he was an old-fashioned warrior who favored the broad-ax and the sword over the musket. He was famous for poking out the eyes and chopping off the arms of captured musketeers because he resented the new realities of modern warfare, in which knights on horseback could be killed by lowly foot soldiers carrying firearms.

A month after Vitelli's appointment, the Signoria engaged the services of a second mercenary, Jacopo d'Appiano, ruler of the Tuscan seaport of Piombino, as well as of the islands of Elba and Monte Cristo. The forty-eight-year-old Jacopo d'Appiano was likewise a veteran *condottiere*, having fought in the past on behalf of Naples, Milan, and Siena. In 1496 he had even fought against Florence on behalf of Pisa. His services were purchased by the Florentines for 25,000 ducats, a large sum considering the city's entire yearly revenues from tolls and other indirect taxes amounted to around 130,000 ducats. Yet Jacopo was dissatisfied with the terms of his contract—he wanted some 5,000 ducats more—and so in March 1499 Machiavelli was ordered to travel to Pontedera, the town twenty miles outside Pisa where Jacopo was encamped. His instructions from the Signoria were of a sort with which he would soon become lamentably familiar. He was to assure Jacopo of Florence's favorable disposition toward his request, but to do so in the vaguest and most general terms so that the Signoria would be under no real obligation to honor it. He was to offer promises, that is, but no money.

For this first diplomatic mission, Machiavelli would have needed to bring all of his rhetorical skills into play. It is revealing that in 1480 his father had borrowed from a Florentine stationer named Zanobi one of the most famous treatises on rhetoric ever written, Cicero's *De oratore*. Whether or not Niccolò read this particular copy (he was only eleven at the time), he would certainly have studied this famous work at a later stage of his education. Cicero described the various qualities that made a good orator as well as the practical exercises he could employ to develop his abilities: training the voice, using gesture, mastering facts, improving the memory, securing the goodwill of the audience, and so forth. Oratorical prowess such as that described by Cicero was highly prized by a Florentine government that (as in their negotiations with Jacopo d'Appiano) always preferred to offer its allies words instead of deeds: Adriani, the First Chancellor, was, after all, a professor of eloquence at the university. Machiavelli's abilities in the gentle art of persuasion—his skills with his tongue as well as his pen—seem to have secured for him not only his important post in the Chancellery but also this ticklish embassy to appease the fractious lord of Piombino.

Even so, Machiavelli's training in eloquence could hardly have prepared him for this mission to a military encampment in the marshy, flood-prone countryside outside Pisa. He would soon become accustomed to the task of riding long distances to justify the ways of a penny-pinching Signoria to grasping warlords moved more by money than by words. Not surprisingly, his first experience with a *condottiere* was not a particularly pleasant one. Jacopo was a crafty politician whose stubborn defiance had once resulted in his excommunication by an angry pope. Nevertheless, the mission turned out to be a success, insofar as Jacopo remained committed to protecting Florence and assaulting Pisa.

Machiavelli seems to have acquitted himself so well, in fact, that a few months later, in the heat of the summer, he was dispatched on an almost identical mission. Leaving behind in the Chancellery what he called "my huge workload," he rode to Forlì, fifty miles northeast of Florence, on the other side of the Apennines. His brief on this occasion was to persuade a third *condottiere*, Ottaviano Riario, to accept a renewal of his contract (which had expired the previous June) without an increase in pay. Or rather, since Ottaviano, who had yet to turn twenty, was away in Milan, Machiavelli was to negotiate with the young mercenary's mother, Caterina Sforza. That Machiavelli should have been sent to deal with so formidable a figure was a measure of the Signoria's faith in their youthful Second Chancellor.

Caterina Sforza was, in her own way, an even more intimidating character than Jacopo d'Appiano. Though only thirty-six, she was already a legendary figure with a tragic and tempestuous history. She was the illegitimate daughter of Galeazzo Maria Sforza, a brutal and licentious Duke of Milan who was murdered by conspirators on the steps of Milan's cathedral in 1476. The violent death of those close to her was something to which Caterina, then aged thirteen, would become horribly accustomed. At fifteen she was married to Girolamo Riario, the nephew of Pope Sixtus IV and the lord of Imola and Forlì. Girolamo was assassinated in 1488, as was, seven years later, her second husband, Giacomo Feo. A third husband, Giovanni de' Medici, a distant cousin of Lorenzo the Magnificent, died in 1498, albeit from natural causes. These tragedies did nothing to dim Caterina's spirits. Nicknamed the Virago, she was notorious for her audacity. She had defied the murderers of her first husband by fleeing alone into the castle of Forlì, and when the assassins threatened to kill her young children if she refused to surrender, she appeared on the ramparts with (according to legend) her skirts raised and her genitals exposed: "I've still got the mold to make others!" she taunted them. More recently she had demonstrated her brand of deadly effrontery by trying to assassinate Pope Alexander VI: she sent him a series of letters enclosed in a cloth that had been wrapped around the head of a plague victim.

With her strawberry-blond hair and porcelain skin, Caterina was as famous for her beauty as for her bravado. She kept a recipe book in which she detailed ingredients for face creams (the same book included recipes for slow-acting poisons). She had been immortalized by the Florentine painter Lorenzo di Credi, and merchants in Forlì did a brisk business selling small drawings of her head. Back at the Chancellery, Machiavelli's friend Biagio Buonaccorsi coveted one of these little souvenirs. "I would like you to send me by return mail a portrait on a sheet of paper of Her Majesty's head, many of which have been done over there. And if you send it," he instructed, "roll it up so that the folds do not spoil it."

Machiavelli for his part seems to have been considerably less enamored of the Virago. He spent almost two weeks in Forlì, negotiations going back and forth as Caterina repeatedly stalled for time, claiming she had no soldiers or gunpowder to spare and making last-minute changes to any agreements. She showed little appreciation for the elegant but empty words that were the cornerstone of so much Florentine diplomacy. Finally, exasperated at the lack of progress, Machiavelli made his dissatisfaction known "in words and gestures" (ones less subtle and polite, no doubt, than those suggested by Cicero) before returning to Florence at the beginning of August. By that point, however, it looked as if Florence was about to succeed in her assault on Pisa, with or without the services of Caterina's soldiers and gunpowder.

"Our campaign in Pisa is going better and better," Biagio Buonaccorsi had written to Machiavelli a few days before the latter returned to Florence. This was no mere wishful thinking. Since his appointment as Florence's military captain a year earlier, Paolo Vitelli had been leading an indecisive campaign of skirmishes with the Pisans that witnessed the mutual raiding of villages, capturing of cattle, destroying of crops, and torching of castles. But as August arrived, Vitelli finally turned his attentions to a direct assault on Pisa itself. Abetted by his older brother, Vitellozzo, his forces promptly captured the nearby stronghold of Ascanio (upon which, Vitelli, according to his custom, amputated the hands of the defenders) and then began bombarding Pisa with 190 cannons. By August 6, his artillery had knocked down forty yards of the wall surrounding the city, and four days later his soldiers stormed Pisa's fortress, putting its military commander to flight. A few days later, on the Feast of the Assumption, his men captured a church and the surrounding neighborhood within the city walls. After almost five years of independence, the rebel city finally appeared to be at the mercy of Florence.

Yet the Signoria was not taking any chances. As the bombardment continued, an order was issued for the Madonna of

Impruneta to be brought to Florence in preparation for Vitelli's assault. The Madonna was Florence's most precious icon. Painted, according to legend, by Saint Luke, it had been discovered buried in the earth in about the year 1000 as the foundations were being dug for the church of Santa Maria, seven miles south of Florence, in Impruneta. The portrait was said to have cried out in pain as the spade struck it; since then the miraculous image had been kept in the church and been carried to Florence—always in a barefoot procession, with the image carefully veiled—in times of need. In the past five years it had been ferried to Florence on at least four different occasions, performing such miracles as the bringing of fine weather for the harvest in 1494 and the bloody massacre in 1496 of forty Pisan soldiers by the people of Livorno.

On this latest occasion, August 24, the procession from Impruneta was interrupted when the portrait became snagged on an olive branch as it was transported through the countryside—a mishap taken by one and all as a good omen. Even so, Pisa failed to capitulate. Rumors that the Pisans were arming themselves with poison arrows gave Vitelli's men pause for thought. Vitelli himself seemed in no mood to press his advantage. The fact that the Great Council of the People had voted against letting him sack the city (and thereby enrich himself and his men with booty) did nothing to whet his appetite for an attack. So recalcitrant was he that suspicions of treachery soon arose—suspicions that his decision to raise the siege at the beginning of September (ostensibly because malaria was decimating his troops) did nothing to allay. This failure was a huge and humiliating blow to Florentine morale. "There was great murmuring throughout Florence," noted one observer.

One person puzzled and enraged by Vitelli's apparently inexplicable failure to take Pisa was Niccolò Machiavelli. If Machiavelli already entertained low opinions of Jacopo d'Appiano and Caterina Sforza, Vitelli's costly vacillations appeared to epitomize the unreliability and double-dealing of those who fought for money instead of patriotic ideals. By abandoning the siege Vitelli was guilty of either cowardice or, far worse, secretly dealing with the enemy. Machiavelli was convinced of the latter. Infuriated by what he called "Vitelli's betrayal," he claimed the failure of the siege "was due to his culpability." The *condottiere*, he wrote, deserved "endless punishment."

This punishment would be meted out soon enough. Vitelli was arrested and brought back to Florence, where he was tortured on the rack and then beheaded on the first of October after he was found guilty at trial (notwithstanding a lack of evidence) of taking bribes from the Pisans. The execution took place on a gallery at the top of the Palazzo della Signoria as the piazza below thronged with people. "It was expected that his head would be thrown down into the piazza," wrote one witness. "It was not thrown down, however, but it was stuck on a spear and shown at the windows of the gallery, with a lighted torch beside it, so that it could be seen by everyone."

A number of Vitelli's close associates, including his doctor, were arrested at the same time; one of them, a man with the angelic name Cherubino, was hanged shortly afterward in the windows of the Palazzo del Podestà. Escaping the clutches of Florentine justice, however, was Paolo's brother, Vitellozzo, a *condottiere* with a well-earned reputation for ferocity. His getaway, along with 200 of his soldiers, was a lapse the Florentines would presently have cause to regret.

Chapter Three

MACHIAVELLI'S TERM AS Second Chancellor was set to expire a few months after the Pisa fiasco. Chancellors were usually elected, in the first instance, to two-year terms, but in 1498 he had been chosen to serve only the remaining twenty months of Alessandro Braccesi's appointment. On January 27, 1500, Machiavelli's name went before the Great Council of the People for the third time in less than two years. The failure to subjugate Pisa must not have counted against him, since he was duly returned to office; this time, as per the regulations, he was elected to a one-year term. He would have been gratified not only by the guarantee of another year's service to the republic but also by the government's payment to him of six gold florins "on account of the dangers he ran." With Pisa not yet subdued, and with outright war having erupted between France and Milan, more dangers undoubtedly lay ahead.

Machiavelli was preparing for a departure to Pisa in May

when his father died. He and Bernardo seem to have been particularly close, sharing a love of books, an interest in politics, and a keen sense of humor. His mother having passed away in 1496, and his two older sisters already married, Niccolò was left alone in the house in Florence with his younger brother, Totto, who was contemplating a career in the Church. Bernardo himself seems not to have been especially religious, though he did donate an altarpiece to a convent so that masses would be said for his soul. He was buried in the Machiavelli tomb in the church of Santa Croce in Florence. Over the next few years a strange and somewhat macabre fraud would take place, as a number of corpses were illicitly interred in this tomb. When a friar from Santa Croce wished to have the interlopers removed, Niccolò's reply was revealing, about both the father and the son: "Well, let them be," Niccolò wrote, "for my father was a great lover of conversation, and the more there are to keep him company, the better pleased he will be."[1]

Machiavelli's government duties left him little enough time to mourn. Barely two months after Bernardo's death, in the middle of July, he set off for France, on a 450-mile journey to Lyons. It was his first trip outside Italy—his first trip, indeed, of more than a few days' ride from Florence. He was given eighty ducats in spending money and a distinguished traveling companion in the person of Francesco della Casa, a former ambassador to France. "You will proceed with all possible haste," read his instructions from the Signoria, which urged him to ride post—to change horses at every inn while he had the strength to do so.[2] This time his mission was to negotiate not with a petty chieftain such as Jacopo d'Appiano but with one of the most powerful men in Europe: King Louis XII of France.

The reason for this expedition was, yet again, the matter of Pisa. At the end of June, ten months after Paolo Vitelli's aborted siege, the Florentines had renewed their attack on the wayward city. This time the troops were composed of Swiss and Gascon mercenaries lent by the French, since Louis XII (who had succeeded Charles VIII in 1498) had promised to restore Pisa to the Florentines in return for a payment of 50,000 ducats. Again, things did not go according to plan. In a dismaying repeat of the events of the previous summer, once the fortifications were partially destroyed by artillery, leaving the way clear, the Swiss and Gascon troops proved no more eager to enter the city than Vitelli's men. These troops in fact behaved worse than Vitelli's soldiers. Many of the Gascons deserted, pillaging as they went. The Swiss acted even more dishonorably: they seized the Florentine commissioner and held him hostage, demanding a ransom.

As Machiavelli had witnessed many of these chaotic and ignominious scenes for himself, he was selected to accompany della Casa to the court of the King of France. The pair of them were to exculpate the Florentines of any blame in the matter and to make it known to the French that the fault lay with the French commander, who had acted, the Signoria stated, with "corruption and cowardice."

Machiavelli and della Casa arrived at the French court in Lyons on July 26, having crossed through the Alps via the pass at Mont Cenis and covered, on average, fifty miles a day. Barely had they arrived in Lyons, however, than the peripatetic nature of the court (whose restlessness reflected Louis XII's passion for hunting red deer as well as his eagerness to escape outbreaks of plague) meant they were obliged to climb back on their horses and ride 125 miles northwest to Nevers, in the heart of Burgundy. Barely had they arrived at Nevers than they were forced to pursue the court ninety miles north to Montargis; and barely had they arrived in Montargis than the court persisted in its stately progress to Melun, near Paris. Soon afterward the court moved a hundred miles west to Blois, more than 700 miles from Florence and (as Agostino Vespucci marveled in a letter to Machiavelli) "almost . . . another world."

Machiavelli and della Casa were not encouraged by their audiences with King Louis and his favorite adviser, Georges d'Amboise, the Cardinal of Rouen. The two Florentine envoys met King Louis and Rouen (whom Machiavelli called "Roano") for the first time at Nevers. The discussions that followed over the next few weeks did nothing to improve relations between Florence and France. King Louis was willing to continue the war against Pisa only so long as the Florentines financed it—and he wanted the Florentines, moreover, to pay the wages of the mutinous Swiss. The Florentines, who needed French help to recapture the city, were powerless to resist his demands, yet the Florentine government merely responded with the sort of vacillation and prevarication that were increasingly the hallmarks of its foreign policy. Machiavelli, no less than the king, was frustrated by these delaying tactics. He pointed out in dispatches to his superiors back home that the French "esteemed only those who are well-armed or those who are willing to pay"—and the Florentines were sadly lacking in both qualities. The fact was that the French, he informed them, "call you Mr. Nobody."

Machiavelli no doubt relished conveying this insult to men with whom he was becoming increasingly exasperated. One of the congenital problems with Florence's government, he had discovered, lay in the revolving door, so to speak, at the Palazzo della Signoria. The eight Signori and their presiding officer, the Gonfalonier of Justice, were elected to two-month terms of office. These drastically abbreviated tenures had come about because only guild members were eligible for office, and limited spells of public service guaranteed they would not be kept unduly from their storerooms and countinghouses. What was good for trade and industry, however, was not so good for politics, since men with little experience or know-how came to serve their short stints in the Palazzo della Signoria; these terms then expired before the men gained any meaningful experience of public affairs. The result was not only a lack of continuity and experience but also an institutionalized dearth of initiative and clear direction on the part of a government that had become fond of uttering such lackluster maxims as "Wise men take what is least bad instead of what is good" and "One ought not to take risks without the most urgent necessity."[3] Particularly at this early stage of his career, such wan adages could hold little appeal for a man like Machiavelli.

It soon became apparent that figures invested with more authority than Machiavelli and della Casa would be required to negotiate with a powerful, if stubborn, ally like Louis XII. But still the Signoria persisted in its policy of foot-dragging, causing an irritated Machiavelli to wait week after week for a Florentine ambassador to depart for France. Not until the middle of December, when word reached him in Nantes that an ambassador was at long last on the way, did a relieved Machiavelli finally receive permission to begin his homeward journey. On the long trip back into Italy he would have had ample time to contemplate the deficiencies of a government that was beholden to its soldiers as well as to the caprices of other rulers, and which based its foreign policy on little more than procrastination and prevarication.

Machiavelli was eager to return to Florence. His friends in the Chancellery missed his exuberant personality, and he must have missed their company as well. In October he had received a letter from Vespucci describing how Biagio and the other secretaries were "all seized by a marvelous desire to see you. For your amusing, witty, and pleasant conversation, while it echoes about our ears, relieves, cheers, and refreshes us." And someone else in Florence, apparently, was likewise looking forward to the return of "Machia." A Chancellery assistant named Andrea di Romolo wrote to him that a certain prostitute near the Ponte alle Grazie was waiting for him "with open figs. . . . You know who I'm talking about."*

---

* Fig (*fico*) is used here as a play on the word *fica*, an Italian slang term for the female sex organs.

Machiavelli arrived back in Florence on January 14, 1501, having been away for a full six months. There was sorrow and anxiety as well as pleasure on his return. His older sister, Primavera, had died during his absence, aged thirty-five. She left behind a husband and a fourteen-year-old son named Giovanni, who was gravely ill as Machiavelli journeyed home. "This is the year of our misfortunes," wrote his disconsolate brother Totto.

There was also the matter of his reelection for Machiavelli to consider: his one-year term would expire at the end of the month, and as far back as October he had been warned by Vespucci that his post would be at risk unless he returned. He was duly returned to office, however, at which point he appealed to his superiors for a well-deserved rest: his private affairs were, he informed them, "in a state of complete disorder."

Chapter Four

THE REGION OF Italy known as the Romagna stretched some ninety miles southeastward from Bologna to the Adriatic coast. It followed the ruler-straight line of the Via Aemilia, an old Roman road, and subsumed a series of fortified cities: Imola, Faenza, Forlì, Cesena, and Rimini, with a jog south to include Urbino and, on the other side of the Apennines, Città di Castello. The Romagna was part of the Papal States, and each of these cities was ruled by a *vicario*, or vicar, in the name of the pope, to whom an annual sum, known as the census, was due. These vicariates were usually kept in the family: the Manfredi clan in Faenza, the Malatesta in Rimini, the Sforza in Pesaro, the Vitelli in Città di Castello. Despite their position as vassals of the pope, many of these vicars possessed a strong independent streak. Their greatest export was war, since most, like the Vitelli, were *condottieri*. What Dante had written two centuries earlier in *The Divine Comedy*—that

"Romagna is not, and it never was / Without war in the heart of its oppressors"[1]—still held horribly true in 1500. Sometimes its tyrants even made war against the pope, as in the case of Sigismondo Malatesta, the "Wolf of Rimini," a violent and impious warlord who had murdered his first two wives and, in 1468, traveled to Rome with the express aim (never accomplished) of murdering Pope Paul II.

These belligerent and self-interested rulers had made the Romagna the weakest link in the Papal States. For centuries it had been a wild and unstable region, vulnerable to foreign aggressors and unreliable in its relations with the pope. The dangers for the papacy had been emphasized most recently by the attempt of Caterina Sforza, ruler of the Romagnol cities of Imola and Forlì, to assassinate Pope Alexander VI, formerly known as Rodrigo Borgia. After the failure of her plot, in March 1499, Alexander had issued a bull expelling from her domains the woman he called a "daughter of iniquity." Her lands were swiftly conquered at the end of 1499 by the pope's twenty-four-year-old son, Cesare Borgia. Caterina had fled into her fortress at Forlì, but this time there was to be no insouciant bravado on the ramparts: her garrison of 400 men was slaughtered, while she herself was captured and taken as a prisoner to Rome.

Caterina Sforza was not the pope's only target. Alexander wished to create a more reliable ally for the Church—and, while he was at it, to found a Borgia dynasty—by installing Cesare as ruler of the entire Romagna. Cesare had been an instrument of his father's ambitions for most of the previous decade. At the age of fifteen he was made Bishop of Pamplona, and at seventeen, one year after his father was elected pope, Cardinal of Valencia. It was a meteoric rise through the ecclesiastical ranks given that he had not taken Holy Orders, and given that, as one chronicler wrote with considerable understatement, he "was totally disinclined toward the sacerdotal profession." He had renounced his cardinalate in 1497, following the murder of his older brother (a death in which many saw Cesare's own hand), in order to embark on a more secular career. In the following year, as a reward for his father having granted King Louis XII a divorce from his wife, he became the Duke of Valentinois (a title that in Italy provided him with the nickname "Valentino"). But both Cesare and his father coveted a more meaningful dukedom than these distant lands along the Rhône in which he had set foot only once.

Citing nonpayment of the census, Alexander VI excommunicated the vicars of Pesaro, Rimini, and Faenza, declaring their lands forfeit to the Church. The next shoe then dropped when in October 1500, while Niccolò Machiavelli was on his legation in France, Cesare Borgia stormed back into the Romagna at the head of an army of 10,000 French and Spanish mercenaries. Pesaro fell without a struggle, followed soon after by Rimini. Only Faenza offered meaningful resistance, but it too eventually fell, following a long siege, in April 1501. Pope Alexander promptly awarded his son the title Duke of Romagna, giving him overlordship of the wayward region.

Cesare Borgia boasted an emphatic new title and a large army with which he had fought two swift and successful military campaigns. Furthermore, he had the backing of both the pope and King Louis XII of France, one of whose relations, Charlotte d'Albret, he had married in 1499. Unsurprisingly, he had an appetite for further conquests. As early as the previous autumn, Agostino Vespucci had reported to Machiavelli, then in France, anxious rumors that Borgia was planning to attack Florence and reinstate the Medici. Matters were made more worrisome by the fact that Borgia had taken into his service Vitellozzo Vitelli, older brother of Paolo. Since swearing revenge on Florence for his brother's death, Vitellozzo had pursued his calling as a mercenary with a savagery distinctly at odds with his cautious behavior outside the walls of Pisa. He had captured and decapitated Pirro da Marciano, brother of Ludovico and the man whom the Florentines had sent to capture him following the Pisa fiasco. Over the next eighteen months he had plundered the territory around Cortona, fought a fierce battle outside the gates of Perugia in which several hundred men had died, and helped Borgia capture Faenza with a contribution of a thousand footsoldiers. His most horrifying spree, in September 1500, saw him sack the small Umbrian city of Acquasparta, burn its castle, and murder and then dismember its ruler, Altobello da Canale.

Most of all, Vitellozzo thirsted for revenge against Florence. Borgia seemed ready to give him satisfaction, since in early May he moved his army into Florentine territory, demanding a free passage across Tuscany to Piombino, from which he was planning to oust Jacopo d'Appiano. Panic gripped Tuscany as Borgia, without awaiting a reply from the Signoria, advanced menacingly in the direction of Florence. As they swarmed through the countryside, his troops began "robbing and committing every sort of cruelty," according to one horror-struck Florentine. Peasants from the countryside were soon packing their most valuable possessions onto beasts of burden and fleeing to within the city walls in fear for their lives.

Florence itself was woefully ill-prepared to deal with the threat, and so ambassadors (accompanied by a group of musicians) were hastily sent to meet Borgia at his camp outside Florence. Bargaining from a position of obvious weakness, the ambassadors capitulated to all of his demands. They agreed to pay him an annual sum of 36,000 ducats, a kind of protection money that amounted, ruinously, to almost a quarter of the city's entire budget. As in 1494, Florence had been resoundingly humbled, its military weaknesses drastically exposed by Borgia's bold predations.

Machiavelli was occupied during these months in 1501 with the affairs of Pistoia, a small city situated on a tributary of the Arno some twenty miles northwest of Florence. Pistoia had been under continuous Florentine rule since the middle of the fourteenth century. Maintaining the peace had never been easy. Pistoia was a violent and dangerous city even by the dreadful standards of the age, with frequent struggles between the two opposing families, the Cancellieri and the Panciatichi. While Machiavelli was away in France, the former had driven the latter from the city amid much looting and killing. The violent disorder then spread beyond the walls of Pistoia, with armed factions battling one another throughout the hilly countryside. These disturbances were referred to euphemistically as *umori*—"moods," or "humors." Early in February, barely a fortnight after returning from France, Machiavelli was sent to the city as a commissioner with wide-ranging powers to halt the *umori* and establish some sort of peace.

This legation did not begin auspiciously. A battle between several thousand Pistoiesi—a significant proportion of the population—left 200 dead only a few days after Machiavelli arrived. He spent ten days in the city before returning to Florence, but by April further battles had killed more than fifty people. At the beginning of July, some 300 died in fighting as the Palazzo Panciatichi was burned to the ground. The heads of a dozen members of the Panciatichi family were stuck on lances and paraded through the city, while other disembodied heads were used for games of *palla*, a primitive version of tennis. Machiavelli was promptly ordered back to Pistoia to arrange another truce.

Machiavelli may well have entertained serious doubts about his mission. More than a decade later he would discuss the three alternative ways of imposing order on a city divided by factions: one could execute the leaders of the factions; or exile them from the city; or force them to lay down their arms and sign a peace agreement. "Of these three ways," he wrote, "this last is most harmful, least certain, and most ineffective"—and yet it was also, he sourly observed, the policy always implemented by Florence in Pistoia. The best method of pacifying a city like Pistoia was, he believed, the first course of action. "But because such decisive actions have in them something great and noble," he pointedly remarked, "a weak republic cannot carry them out."

Yet another slaughter took place during Machiavelli's second visit to Pistoia. A conciliation of sorts soon took place before the end of summer, with each faction electing four men to Pistoia's Signoria; but the peaceful state of affairs lasted only a week before further violence erupted. By that time, Machiavelli was back in Florence with other business to attend to. At the age of thirty-two, he was about to get married.

Machiavelli's bride was Marietta Corsini. Virtually nothing is known of the details of their marriage—not even the precise date of the wedding—and only slightly more about Marietta herself. Like Machiavelli, she was a member of a somewhat down-at-heels branch of an old Florentine family from the minor nobility: the Corsini were a noble clan from the area around Poggibonsi, south of Florence, but in the middle of the fourteenth century they had been ruined by the failure of the Florentine banks of Peruzzi and Bardi. The family's most illustrious member had been Andrea Corsini, a fourteenth-century bishop of Fiesole who had received a vision of the Virgin Mary, and who would later, in 1629, be canonized.

It is safe to assume the marriage was not, first and foremost, a love match. Of greater importance to a man was the size of a woman's dowry and—for the purposes of childbearing—the size of her hips. Machiavelli's marriage would have been the upshot of negotiations between himself and Marietta's father, Luigi, and brother, Lanciolino. Nuptials in Florence were often arranged by marriage brokers, involving a series of agreements that were documented in legal contracts and ritualized ceremonially. One such ceremony was the *impalmamento*, in which the groom, signifying his intention to marry, took the hand of his prospective bride in the presence of witnesses. There then followed the *sponsalia*, in which the male members of the two families came together to discuss vital financial matters such as the dowry and the cost of the bride's dress. The final stage was the *nozze*, when, after the wedding mass, the bride was led in procession to the house of her new husband.

Sometime in the late summer of 1501, Marietta would have been delivered to the house in the Via della Piazza (the present Via Guicciardini), near the south end of the Ponte Vecchio. Her new home was part of a complex of three or four houses, all occupied by Niccolò's relations, that dated from the middle of the fourteenth century. The houses backed onto an enclosure, shaded by a loggia, known as the *cortile di Machiavelli*, or "Machiavelli Court." Niccolò had at least one servant, and his house included storerooms on the ground floor for wine and grain, bedrooms and living rooms on the first floor, and a kitchen at the top. Behind his house a smaller two-story property, accessible through an alley, was used to accommodate the servants. Like most houses in Florence, his home had iron bars on the windows—a feature intended to keep thieves out and the womenfolk in.*

---

* The Machiavelli house—long since demolished—stood at what is now no. 16, via Guicciardini.

The bars on the windows would indeed make the Casa Machiavelli seem a prison to Marietta, and on more than one occasion she had reason to deplore her fate. Machiavelli would make a far from ideal husband. No doubt he subscribed, like most every other Italian male, to the precepts in Bernardo Machiavelli's most expensive book, Gratian's *Decretum*, which announced that "women should be subject to their men" and that "women's authority is nothing." More recently, the humanist scholar Leonardo Bruni, one of Machiavelli's predecessors in the Chancellery, had written of male power in equally uncompromising terms: "The man is head of the household, the king, so to speak, of his own home."

Machiavelli's problem seems not to have been his authoritarianism so much as the fact that he was frequently inattentive and, as we shall see, more than occasionally unfaithful, consorting over the years with both prostitutes and mistresses. Many years later, a friend would write to him: "You would never have married if you had really known yourself." Machiavelli claimed to envy bachelors, and in his writings he could be unsentimental, and even cynical, about marriage. "Every man who has a mistress," he later wrote, "is distressed at being given a wife." Another of his works, a novella, would open with the god of the Underworld reflecting on how most damned souls blamed their afflictions on the horrors of married life. Still another, his commentary on Livy, was to conclude with the image of the women of ancient Rome poisoning their husbands. As for Marietta herself, she seems to have been an intelligent and caring (if somewhat high-strung) woman who genuinely en-

41

joyed her husband's company and missed him deeply whenever his duties for the government took him away from Florence.

As it happened, business took Machiavelli away from the marital home almost immediately. In October he was off on horseback to deal yet again with the warring factions in Pistoia. Soon afterward, Marietta discovered she was pregnant. Machiavelli had no time to play the doting husband, even if he wished to. The following year, possibly right around the time Marietta gave birth to their daughter, he was dispatched on a much more important mission: he was to represent Florence at the court of Cesare Borgia.

Chapter Five

A YEAR ON from his conquest of the Romagna and his harrowing of Florence, Cesare Borgia was flush with yet another victory. He had conquered the dukedom of Urbino in June 1502 by means of a typically daring and treacherous deception. Appealing to the city's ruler, Guidobaldo da Montefeltro, for help in conquering Camerino, he promptly invaded Urbino with 2,000 Spanish mercenaries after the hapless Guidobaldo faithfully sent along his artillery to besiege Camerino. It was his most stunning triumph yet, one that made him master of the wealthy and beautiful city that had been ruled by the Montefeltro family since the middle of the twelfth century. The conquest also made him, indisputably, a force to be reckoned with by the other Italian powers.

The Florentines certainly took note of his dangerous new prominence. Once again fearful rumors abounded that Florence was next on Borgia's list, and so, when on the eve of entering Urbino he requested the presence of ambassadors with whom to discuss weighty matters of territorial alliances, the Signoria did not hesitate. Niccolò Machiavelli was dispatched straightaway, along with a member of a venerable Florentine family, Francesco Soderini, the Bishop of Volterra. They arrived at the Palazzo Ducale in Urbino on the evening of June 24, the Feast of San Giovanni, and were immediately summoned by Borgia.

In the summer of 1502, Florence was once more in a position of great vulnerability. The campaign against Pisa was proceeding as miserably as ever: that spring the Florentines had dispatched teams of marauders, known as *marraiuoli* (from *marra*, "pickax"), to lay waste to the Pisan countryside, but the Pisans had captured the *marraiuoli*, had hanged, drawn, and quartered them, and then began taking their own pickaxes to the crops and orchards in Florentine territory. Worse still, at the beginning of June a rebellion broke out in Arezzo, a city under Florentine control since 1384. The rebellious Aretini had summoned Vitellozzo Vitelli, who was conveniently on hand with several thousand troops. Relishing his revenge against his brother's killers, the *condottiere* swiftly seized strongholds in the Val di Chiana and then entered Arezzo as a liberator. Despite Borgia's protests that he knew nothing of Vitellozzo's maneuvers, few in Florence failed to see the hand of Duke Valentino in the affair. But the Florentines were, as usual, powerless to mount a vigorous response.

Such was the state of play when Machiavelli and Bishop Soderini came face-to-face with Cesare Borgia in the magnificent Palazzo Ducale in Urbino. Though Borgia was despised and feared in Florence, Machiavelli formed a particularly favorable view of him. His lurid reputation notwithstanding, Borgia was in fact an accomplished and impressive young man. He had proved himself an irreproachable student, receiving a solid education at both the university in Perugia and at Machiavelli's old school, the Studio Fiorentino in Pisa. He was fluent in five languages, among them Latin and Greek, though he was much more at home in the saddle and the bullring (on one memorable day in Rome he had slain eight bulls) than in the classroom. He could break a horseshoe with his bare hands, and his spare time in Urbino was spent hunting with leopards in the surrounding hills and challenging the local youths to footraces and wrestling matches, all of which, invariably, he won. He dressed in suits of black velvet and frequently wore a mask—for the sake of inscrutability and anonymity as much as for concealment of the disfiguring symptoms of syphilis.

"This prince is very splendid and magnificent," an awed Machiavelli wrote to the members of the Signoria soon after his arrival in Urbino. Yet it was not Borgia's strength and athleticism, nor even his facility in Latin or Greek, that struck Machiavelli. What Machiavelli admired from the outset was Borgia's unfaltering resolution and the breathtaking audacity of his actions. "In war," Machiavelli wrote to his superiors, "there is no great enterprise that does not seem small to him, and in his pursuit of glory and gains he never knows rest or fears danger or weariness. He arrives in one place before it is known he left the previous one. His soldiers love him, and he has gathered around him the best men in Italy. Such things make him victorious and formidable." A more pronounced contrast with the hesitant and wavering members of the Signoria—businessmen who understood the price of wool but not the art of war—would have been difficult to imagine.

Borgia treated the two representatives from Florence with the same highhandedness and contempt shown by the King of France. He threatened to change the Florentine government, specifically, to reinstate Piero de' Medici, unless the Signoria pledged to respect his conquests and forbear meddling in his affairs. He also brought up the small matter of the 36,000 ducats that the Florentines had so far neglected to pay. "If you will not have me as a friend," he warned, "then you shall have me as an enemy." The nocturnal interview terminated with Borgia urging the two men to impress their bosses in Florence with the urgency of his requests. "Make your decision speedily," he told them that night, the next day delivering his ultimatum: that the Florentines had four days to decide whether Borgia was their friend or their foe. "There can be," he stated, "no middle way."

As he galloped back across the rugged hills to report Borgia's demands to the Signoria, Machiavelli must have been painfully aware that the middle way, what they called *la via di mezzo*, was precisely the path his cautious government preferred to tread. Predictably, the Signoria declined to respond to Borgia's urgent demands. In the first week of July, several days after the expiration of the deadline, the government merely delivered to Urbino one of its usual masterpieces of empty eloquence. Borgia's fury upon the receipt of the document prompted Bishop Soderini to flee Urbino in fear for his life, but events soon played in Florence's favor. The members of the Signoria must have suspected Borgia's harsh ultimatum to be a bluff, especially since King Louis XII would hardly countenance an invasion of Florence, with whom he had signed a treaty only a few months earlier. His bluff was called, ironically, when Vitellozzo Vitelli captured and sacked the Tuscan town of Borgo San Sepolcro, a dozen miles northeast of Arezzo, and then carried out a brutal massacre at the fortress of Battifolle. Louis XII was highly displeased with these events, and so Borgia was forced to order his malicious lieutenant out of Tuscany. An enraged Vitellozzo duly withdrew his troops (and, while he was at it, stole the bells from the citadel). By the end of July he was swearing vengeance against Borgia as well as against the Florentines.

The crisis had passed. The Florentines had survived their second confrontation with Cesare Borgia in little more than a year. However, those experiences had left their mark on the members of the Signoria. Recognizing the inherent weakness in their way of doing business, of rapidly rotating through office men who had an extremely limited experience of political affairs, they decided to make an important institutional reform. Rather than electing a Gonfalonier of Justice who would serve a term of only two months, they proposed the creation of an office called the *Gonfaloniere a vita*, or Gonfalonier for Life, a permanent position that (like the Doge in Venice) would bring to the Republic a greater continuity and stability as well as a political wisdom born of experience.

Accordingly, a law instituting this new office was passed at the end of August, and a fortnight later the names of 236 candidates were sent before the Great Council of the People. The Madonna of Impruneta was, according to custom, carried into Florence to help the voters make a wise choice. The ballots were cast, and the victor to emerge was a veteran statesman named Piero Soderini, a former ambassador to both Milan and France. The fifty-two-year-old Soderini was the brother of Francesco, the Bishop of Volterra, the envoy with whom Machiavelli had gone to Urbino. Francesco had clearly admired and valued Machiavelli's talents, insights, and courage during their legation, writing soon afterward that the Second Chancellor was "second to none in ability." Piero, too, would quickly come to depend on Machiavelli's skills. He had been in office less than a month, in fact, when he sent his Second Chancellor on another mission. As Cesare Borgia's neighbors nervously awaited his next move, the Florentines realized they needed someone to keep a close eye on him. Machiavelli was to get a second chance to observe the "splendid" duke at close quarters.

Machiavelli took to this latest assignment with gusto. Urged by the government to move swiftly, he began traveling with his baggage in a coach. But soon finding himself weighed down by these accessories, he abandoned them at Scarperia, fifteen miles outside of Florence, and rode post for the remaining twenty-five miles to Imola, where Cesare Borgia was holding court. He arrived on October 7, and presented himself to Borgia while still in his riding clothes.

A change had taken place in Borgia's fortunes since Machiavelli had seen him three months earlier in Urbino. The Duke of Romagna suddenly looked vulnerable as the disgruntled Vitellozzo Vitelli and a number of other *condottieri* who had assisted in Borgia's conquest of the Romagna (including the lords of Perugia and Fermo) gathered in Perugian territory to discuss how to defeat the ambitious overlord. The devious ousting of Guidobaldo da Montefeltro had alerted them to the jeopardy of their own situations. As Gianpaolo Baglioni, ruler of Perugia, expressed it, they risked "being one by one swallowed by the dragon." Two days after Machiavelli arrived at Imola, on October 9, the rebel *condottieri* signed a pact agreeing to attack Borgia simultaneously in the Romagna and at Urbino, the latter of which was already in revolt against his rule.

Despite these setbacks, Borgia appeared no less magnificent to Machiavelli. The duke was, as Machiavelli wrote to the Ten, "superhuman in his courage." Faced with the possibility of losing his territorial gains, he began appealing to both Florence and the King of France for assistance. In the meantime he started recruiting a citizen militia with which to counter Vitellozzo and the other defecting mercenaries, conscripting one man from each household in the surrounding Romagnol villages and eventually putting together a force of 6,000 men. He dressed them in uniforms that included a crimson-and-yellow smock emblazoned CESARE.

Machiavelli was impressed by both this militia and the sangfroid with which Borgia contemplated his enemies, whom he dismissed as a "congress of failures." Writing to the Signoria, Machiavelli urged his government to support Borgia against this group of petty tyrants. The Duke of Romagna was, he wrote, "highly reputed, favored by Fortune, and accustomed to winning"—not to mention the fact that he had behind him both the pope's money and Louis XII's soldiers. Florence would do well, he believed, to make a friend rather than an enemy of this "new power in Italy."

At first it seemed the Florentine government would take this advice. In the third week of October, Machiavelli received a letter from Piero Guicciardini, a member of the Ten of Liberty and Peace, assuring him that "a favourable disposition is to be seen in everyone toward friendship with His Lordship there." Typically, the government equivocated. Borgia was offered words of encouragement from Florence but little in the way of material support. Irritatingly for Machiavelli, Piero Soderini seemed more interested in the fate of some mules seized by Borgia's men from a mule train in Castel Durante, near Urbino. The Gonfalonier was strangely obsessed with these beasts. "You will come with His Excellency to the specific case of the six mules that were taken," Soderini wrote to him with stern emphasis. "You will beseech him for this *over and over again*."

Machiavelli's time in Imola gradually stretched into November and then December as both the Signoria and the rebel mercenaries, who showed no special appetite for battle, continued their dithering. Back in Florence, Machiavelli's young wife began to fret. "Madonna Marietta wrote to me via her brother to ask when you will be back," Biagio Buonaccorsi had written in October. "She is making a big fuss, and she is hurt because you promised her you would stay eight days and no more." By December she had grown even more furious and disconsolate: "Madonna Marietta is cursing God," Biagio reported, "and she feels she has thrown away both her body and her possessions."

Machiavelli, for his part, soon longed to return home. He was worried, once again, that his absence from Florence would jeopardize his reelection to the Chancellery. He was also frustrated by both Borgia's secrecy and the Signoria's dawdling. Evidently bored by the long days of inactivity, he asked Biagio to find him a copy of Plutarch's *Lives* with which to while away the hours. (He usually traveled with books in his saddlebags: his reading material on the long trek to France had been Julius Caesar's *Commentaries on the Gallic and Civil Wars*.) He also wrote to Florence, requesting a velvet-and-damask cloak and a new velvet hat (evidently he wished to cut a better appearance at Borgia's court) and a shipment of wine. In return he received petty and sometimes harassing letters. "Go scratch your ass," Biagio wrote back ill-temperedly. "You can go to the devil for asking so many things." Biagio also informed him that his reports were not arriving as regularly as the Signoria wished. "I must remind you to write more often," he scolded Machiavelli at the end of October, "because the passage of 8 days at a time between the arrival of your letters does not bring you honor, nor much satisfaction to those who sent you." Some of his reports went astray, while others, thanks to the leisurely progress of the couriers, took more than a week to travel the forty miles from Imola to Florence. "That asshole Totti took 8 full days getting here," griped a frustrated Biagio. Still, the Chancellery itself was hardly more effectual. At one point a safe-conduct for Machiavelli arrived late in Imola because, as Biagio freely admitted, one of the officials, Antonio della Valle, had spent the entire day playing backgammon when he should have been preparing the document.

Machiavelli had spent two months in Imola when, on December 10, ploughing through heavy snow, Borgia left the city with a force of 5,000 infantry and 1,200 cavalry. His first destination was Cesena, thirty miles to the southeast. Machiavelli followed two days later, wondering, like everyone else, what Borgia was planning. As it turned out, the duke's first action was a grisly *coup de théâtre* that shocked and mesmerized Machiavelli no less than anyone else.

One of Borgia's closest associates for many years had been a saturnine, black-bearded Spaniard named Ramiro de Lorqua who had enjoyed wide-ranging powers as military governor of the Romagna. Ramiro had made himself brutally effective but widely unpopular by pacifying the region and squelching all dissent toward Borgia's lordship. His career came to an abrupt end as dawn broke on December 26 and the people of Cesena gathered in the city's piazza to witness Borgia's Christmas gift to them: the decapitated corpse of Ramiro lying exposed, the head stuck on a lance, a bloodstained ax and execution block sitting nearby. "No one knows the reason for his death," Machiavelli wrote to his superiors, "except that it has suited the

Prince, who shows how he can create and destroy men as he pleases."

The bloody corpse of Ramiro was only the opening act. Later the same day Borgia set off with his army for Senigallia, on the Adriatic coast, where his enemies, Vitellozzo Vitelli among them, were lying in wait.

Chapter Six

THE REBEL *condottieri* of the Romagna possessed a sobering record of violence and treachery. Gianpaolo Baglioni had been the instigator of the ruthless massacre of 130 members of the rival Oddi family in Perugia. Equally appalling had been the career of twenty-seven-year-old Oliverotto Eufferducci. He had been raised by his maternal uncle, Giovanni Fogliani, the ruler of Fermo, a small city in the Marches. Entering military service, he fought against Pisa with Paolo Vitelli in the ill-fated 1499 Florentine campaign, escaping Paolo's fate thanks only to the timely intervention of his uncle. Oliverotto repaid his uncle's kindness two years later by murdering him at a banquet in Fermo and seizing control of the city.

Despite their well-deserved reputations for savagery, these men had proved themselves tentative and incompetent when it came to dealing with Borgia. Vitellozzo Vitelli's resolution was not improved by his syphilitic condition: he had been carried into the conference at La Magione on a stretcher, groaning in pain. No meaningful military action was taken after the compact was signed, and indeed a number of the *condottieri* even began making peaceful overtures. Machiavelli was puzzled by these approaches, wondering how their sins against Borgia could ever be forgiven. Borgia, for his part, had merely bided his time until, at the end of November 1502, he signed a peace treaty with their representatives. A month later, on the same day that Ramiro de Lorqua met his end, the *condottieri*, pretending to show their allegiance, captured Senigallia in Borgia's name. Vitellozzo and Oliverotto then entered the city, supposedly to pay their respects to Borgia as soon as he arrived. Machiavelli, who followed Borgia to Senigallia, would call what happened next "the most beautiful deception."

Machiavelli would later write that Borgia's "powers of dissimulation" fooled the *condottieri* into believing he was their ally. Yet men as murderously faithless as Vitellozzo and Oliverotto would not have been so unwise as to believe that Borgia, an equally merciless character, would ever forgive them their sins or respect the terms of the peace treaty. In fact, they were almost certainly planning to murder Borgia as soon as he set foot in Senigallia. They claimed the castellan of the citadel would surrender the fortress to no one but Borgia, thus luring him to Senigallia; a crossbowman would do the rest. Borgia seems to have caught wind of this rather obvious conspiracy, but he nevertheless met Vitellozzo, who was on muleback, outside the gates of Senigallia on the last day of 1502. There followed friendly greetings and then a splendidly choreographed maneuver the result of which was that Vitellozzo and Oliverotto found themselves inside Senigallia with Borgia and many of his troops, but with most of their own soldiers, in a fatally stupid oversight, outside the walls. The two *condottieri* were promptly arrested and, hours later, strangled by Borgia's right-hand man, Miguel da Corella, a fearsome Spaniard known as Don Michelotto. Thus ended what Borgia later called "their infinite perfidy and malignity."

The ambush and murder of Vitellozzo and Oliverotto may have been a minor event in Italian politics, but in Machiavelli's imagination it would loom large for many years to come. He himself was present in Senigallia on the night of the executions and confessed himself to being "lost in wonder" at Borgia's brilliant masterstroke. He admired the qualities of leadership shown by Borgia throughout the crisis: the fearless determination to destroy his enemies, the clever subterfuge, the panache with which the plan was executed, and the way in which, instead of relying on committees of advisors, he "controls everything by himself" and was therefore able to act swiftly and suddenly.

Still enthralled by these events, soon after returning to Florence on January 23 he composed a 2,500-word chronicle of the event entitled *Description of the Methods Adopted by the Duke Valentino When Murdering Vitellozzo Vitelli, Oliverotto da Fermo, and Others.* The account was not without a certain poetic license: Machiavelli has Vitellozzo asking for his sins to be pardoned and (perhaps less fancifully) Oliverotto blaming Vitellozzo for everything. But the work was more than a literary exercise or a mere record of events. It was an analysis of the way in which a courageous and resourceful leader could outwit and relentlessly crush his enemies. A small fragment of history was offered up as an object lesson, as a profitable example of how a man of talent and ability could snatch triumph from the jaws of jeopardy. Important lessons in statecraft and leadership were to be learned, Machiavelli believed, from the actions taken by Cesare Borgia in the last months of 1502. In this brief account, one can see the germination of an idea that would find its fuller expression a decade later, in the work that would make Machiavelli, in his own way, as feared and mistrusted as Borgia.

Cesare Borgia's reign was not to last. "This month is fatal for fat men," his obese father, Pope Alexander VI, observed morosely at the beginning of August 1503. It certainly proved so in his case, since two weeks later he was dead, probably of malaria. During the same week, his son Cesare fell desperately ill with a fever so intense he ordered his men to submerge him neck deep in ice water. This illness, together with the death of his father, meant Borgia's territorial gains of the past eighteen months were swiftly eroded. Less than a month after Alexander's funeral, the Vitelli had returned to power in Città di Castello, Jacopo d'Appiano reclaimed Piombino, and Guidobaldo da Montefeltro was again in residence at the Palazzo Ducale in Urbino. Worse was to come, and before the end of the year Borgia was faced with a much more guileful and dangerous enemy than the vicars of the Romagna.

Alexander VI had been succeeded in September by Pope Pius III; but Pius died after a reign of only twenty-six days, and another conclave was assembled at the end of October. Machiavelli went to Rome, his first-ever visit to the city, to report on events for the Signoria. Leaving behind his heavily pregnant wife (Marietta had already given birth to their daughter, Primerana, the previous year), he arrived on October 27, 1503, in time to witness the demolition of the man he had esteemed as an exemplary political leader.

Machiavelli reported back to Florence how several prominent candidates were courting Borgia because of his influence (thanks to his Iberian blood) with the Spanish cardinals. The successful suitor turned out to be a powerful cardinal named Giuliano della Rovere, who signed a pact with Borgia pledging both to retain him as Captain-General of the Church (a post he held under his father) and to help restore his lands in the Romagna. Borgia duly delivered the Spanish vote, and on November 1, 1503, the fifty-nine-year-old Cardinal della Rovere began his reign as Pope Julius II.

Machiavelli suspected that Borgia, hitherto a brilliant tactician, had just committed a grave blunder. "The Duke lets himself get carried away by his tremendous confidence," he wrote, "believing the words of others are worth more than his own." In fact, Julius undoubtedly had little intention of keeping to his part of the bargain. He and Cesare's father, Pope Alexander VI, had been mortal enemies: one of Alexander's first acts upon entering the Vatican in 1492 was to try to serve a cup of poison to his rival. Cardinal della Rovere had then fled

Rome and spent an unhappy decade exiled in France, plotting the destruction of his enemy. Machiavelli reported the gossip that the new pope's "innate hatred" of Cesare was notorious. "It cannot be supposed," he remarked, "that Julius II will have forgotten the ten years of exile which he was forced to suffer under Alexander VI." Julius had indeed not forgotten, and retribution came swiftly to Borgia. By the third week of November he was stripped of his title Duke of Romagna and ordered to hand over the keys and passwords to his castles, all of which, the pope insisted, were the property of the Church. When he refused, Julius had him arrested and imprisoned. Duke Valentino's reign of terror was at an end.

Julius's stratagem neatly duplicated Borgia's treatment of the rebel *condottieri* a year earlier. Borgia's downfall was widely celebrated, not least in Florence, where he was said to have been "paid in full for his cruelties." Still, such shameless deception— breaking a pact while its ink was still wet—generally attracted moral shudders. Dante, for example, had taken a dim view of all political deceit, asking rhetorically: "What good man would ever seek gain by means of force or fraud?"[1] Accordingly, in *The Divine Comedy* he placed Guido da Montefeltro, a notorious breaker of oaths and contracts, in the Eighth Circle of Hell, where he was imprisoned inside an eternal flame as punishment for his "subtle ways of acting under cover."[2] Dante would certainly have condemned Julius's subtle ways, but Machiavelli, the man later abominated for pointing out that princes must know how to be liars and deceivers, was more measured in his judgment. "We see that this Pope is beginning to pay his debts honorably," he wrote with sarcasm dripping from his quill. "He wipes them out with the cotton-wool from the inkstand." If he regretted, on one level, the downfall of his hero, he took note of the unflinching and unscrupulous attitude of the pope, a leader who, like Borgia, was willing to use both force and fraud to achieve his ends. With one teacher of political lessons vanished from the scene, another had arrived to take his place.

The downfall of Cesare Borgia was a source of curiosity and bafflement to Machiavelli. Borgia seemed to have done everything possible, in Machiavelli's opinion, to lay the foundations for a long and successful rule. He had wiped out many of his enemies; he had ruled the Romagna with strength and efficiency; he had conscripted a fighting force from among his own subjects; he had won influence and favor at both the Vatican and the French courts; and he had enjoyed a good deal of clout in the College of Cardinals. Yet his reign lasted only a couple of years. How, then, did it all go wrong? What were the causes of his downfall, and what, if anything, could he have done differently?

In order to understand and explain Borgia's unhappy fate, Machiavelli turned to an astrologer. The practice of astrology was as widespread in Florence as in the rest of Europe. Few rulers in the fifteenth century had dared lay the cornerstone of a palace or a church, sign a treaty, hire a *condottiere*, or even dedicate the high altar of a cathedral, without first checking with an astrologer for reassurance. Charles VIII of France, for instance, had taken the precaution of consulting his astrologer,

Simon Phares, before invading Italy in 1494; and despite his tremendous belief in his own abilities, Borgia was equally in the thrall of astrology. He had employed several practitioners, one of whom, a Spaniard named Gaspar Torrella, was also, handily enough, an expert in the treatment of syphilis. During the crisis of the *condottieri*, these astrologers had satisfied Borgia that the stars indicated 1502 to be, as he blithely informed Machiavelli, "a bad year for subjects to rebel against their rulers." That prediction may well have been proved true, but the year 1503 had apparently been less fortunate for tyrants.

Machiavelli no less than anyone else was caught up in what Savonarola—one of astrology's few opponents—called this "pestiferous fallacy." His forensic analyses of historical and political events were undergirded by a faith in the prevailing assumption that the motions of the heavens could influence and even control events on earth. But what was the precise relation, he wished to know, between human actions and these astrological events? Had Borgia's fate been written in the stars, thereby making his defeat inescapable? Was man merely the passive plaything of otherworldly forces that predetermined his fate? Or was it possible for him to oppose these celestial influences and exercise a freedom of will and action?

These philosophical questions were much on Machiavelli's mind in the months following Borgia's collapse. For answers he turned to Bartolomeo Vespucci, professor of astronomy at the University of Padua and the author of a treatise titled *In Praise of Astrology*. Sometime in the first few months of 1504 he wrote a letter to Vespucci, a Florentine, asking if it was possible for a man to resist the influence of the stars. Vespucci wrote back at the beginning of June, reassuring him that "all the ancients proclaimed with one voice that the wise man himself is able to alter the influences of the stars." Vespucci was no doubt alluding to, among others, Aristotle, who argued in his *Magna moralia* (Great Ethics) that the stars had control over the "external goods" of man (parents, friends, wealth, physical strength, personal appearance) but not over the intellectual and moral virtues that he called the "goods of the soul." Astrological determinism had been refuted more recently by Saint Thomas Aquinas, who wrote in his *Summa theologiae* that "the astrologers themselves are wont to say that 'the wise man rules the stars' forasmuch, namely, as he rules his own passions."

The jurisdiction of the stars had been attacked even more recently by Giovanni Pico, the Count of Mirandola, one of the brightest intellectual stars in the circle of Lorenzo the Magnificent. In a treatise published posthumously in 1496, *Disputations Against Astrology*, Pico had denied the stars any influence whatsoever over the mind of man, which was subject, he claimed, to neither time nor space. Man had the freedom to think—and therefore to act—independently of how the constellations disposed themselves. As Vespucci put it, man had the freedom and ability to choose his path, "changing his own step, now one way and now another."

By 1504 the idea that a rational man could avert the influence of the stars was so widespread that Machiavelli's question must have struck Vespucci as naïve, perhaps even somewhat ignorant. Be that as it may, Vespucci had given Machiavelli license to imagine a world in which men were free to oppose the dictates of their horoscopes and make themselves masters of their own fates. Over the next few years Machiavelli would continue to contemplate the outcome of Borgia's career within this context, together with the possibilities of combating destinies that had been written in the stars.

Chapter Seven

MACHIAVELLI HAD RETURNED to Florence in the middle of December 1503, following almost eight weeks in Rome. Marietta had given birth to their second child during his absence: a son, christened Bernardo in honor of Niccolò's father. "He is hairy like you," Marietta wrote, adding tenderly: "Since he looks like you, he seems beautiful to me." A friend named Luca Ugolini happily confirmed this likeness: "Your Madonna Marietta did not deceive you, for he is your spitting image. Leonardo da Vinci would not have done a better portrait." However, Biagio Buonaccorsi warned that, as usual, the high-strung Marietta was anxious for her husband to return. "She lives in great distress about this absence of yours," he reported to Machiavelli in mid-November, then a fortnight later sighed in exasperation: "Good Lord, there is no way to get her to calm down and take comfort." Machiavelli, though, seems to have been in no special hurry to see either his wife or his new son. Ordered by the Ten early in December to return forthwith to Florence, he managed by various excuses to prolong his stay by another two weeks. One of his pleasures in the Eternal City was singing with friends to the accompaniment of a bowed string instrument called a rebec.

His wife and young children were not the only ones whom Machiavelli neglected during his sojourn in Rome. To the dismay of Biagio, Machiavelli could be equally delinquent in his dealings with his superiors in the Signoria. In November he had received a letter from a member of the Signoria, Agnolo Tucci, a paper merchant, requesting a report about Julius II's policy in the Romagna. When the letter was met with an insulting silence, Tucci became furious, condemning Machiavelli in a meeting of the Signoria with expressions, reported Biagio, "that were indeed of a bad nature." To make matters worse, no one had sprung to Machiavelli's defense; the other members of the Signoria, according to Biagio, had simply nodded approvingly at this invective.

Machiavelli finally bestirred himself to reply, penning a letter to Tucci that was a masterpiece of condescension. Taking swipes at the paper merchant's supposedly poor handwriting and his lack of knowledge of Latin, he made clear his disdain: Tucci was an amateur politician whose petty demands and limited experience of public affairs were irksome to a well-seasoned expert such as himself. Biagio would soon caution Machiavelli that he needed to flatter the vanities of his superiors in the Palazzo della Signoria, "because everyone wants to be coddled and esteemed, so that is what someone who finds himself where you are has to do. A few kind words with a couple of notices will give satisfaction." Machiavelli, however, seems to have been unable to suffer fools gladly or—ironically, considering the lessons he had just learned from Cesare Borgia—to exercise his powers of dissimulation.

Tucci's denunciation did not hinder Machiavelli's career, since he was reappointed to the Chancellery a month after returning to Florence. An important legation, his second to France, then beckoned at the end of January. Three years after his last visit, and nine years since Charles VIII's invasion, French fortunes in Italy had reached a sorry pass. Louis XII claimed not only the French throne but also those of Naples and Jerusalem. If the latter was wishful thinking in the extreme, in the previous few years he had come close to realizing his ambitions in Naples. In 1500 he and King Ferdinand II of Aragón signed the Treaty of Granada, agreeing to depose King Federigo IV (who happened to be Ferdinand's cousin) and partition the Kingdom of Naples between them. This objective was easily accomplished a year later, but disagreement over the terms of the Treaty of Granada resulted in war between the signatories in the summer of 1502. The French achieved several early victories, but in 1503 Gonsalvo de Córdoba, known as *El Gran Capitán*, inflicted two devasting defeats on Louis XII's forces, one at Cerignola, seventy-five miles northeast of Naples, and a second and final one on the banks of the river Garigliano. French power in Naples had reached a bloody and emphatic end.

Machiavelli's latest mission to France, in 1504, was directly connected to these events. He was to confirm Louis XII's willingness to protect Florence from the Spaniards—a grave new threat in Italy—in the event that Córdoba moved his army north to claim Tuscany for King Ferdinand. Traveling in the dead of winter, he was received at the court in Lyons by his old sparring partner, the Cardinal of Rouen. The all-powerful Roano listened to his appeals with displeasure—the French had problems enough of their own without fretting over the fate of Florence—but ultimately eased Florentine anxieties with news of a truce between France and Spain. With this problem solved (though only temporarily, as it happened), Machiavelli returned to Florence in the middle of March. His attention then shifted to other business: the ever-present problem of Pisa.

By the spring of 1504, Pisa had enjoyed almost a decade of independence from Florence. The malcontents showed little indication of returning to the fold anytime soon, though in May the Florentines enjoyed a rare success when they captured the fortress of Ripafratta. Plans were then made for an all-out assault on the rebel city until word reached Florence that the Pisans taken prisoner at Ripafratta claimed that inside the walls of Pisa were 2,000 well-armed fighters in addition to 500 infantry and 300 light cavalry financed by Siena and Lucca. The Florentine will to fight, never very robust in the first place, rapidly wilted. Instead, an ingenious new plan was set in motion. In July the members of the Signoria voted for work to begin on a massive engineering project: to divert the course of the Arno, leaving Pisa, quite literally, high and dry.

There was a disconcerting precedent for this Florentine plan to press hydraulic engineering into the service of warfare. In 1430 the architect Filippo Brunelleschi had attempted to subdue Lucca by constructing a dam across the river Serchio, thereby flooding the surrounding countryside and leaving the Lucchesi stranded in the middle of a lake. Unfortunately for the Florentine war effort, the dam was breached by the Lucchesi, causing the Florentine camp to flood and a humiliated Brunelleschi to beat a hasty retreat to higher ground. Undaunted by this experience, the Florentines now proposed to dig a canal twelve miles long and thirty feet deep in order to redirect the Arno—the lifeblood of the Pisans—into a stagnant swampland six miles south of Pisa. Like the Lucchesi, the Pisans would be cut off, for all intents and purposes, from the outside world. And whereas the great Brunelleschi had directed the 1430 effort, this time the initiative would be taken by a man whose reputation for technical wizardry approached that of Brunelleschi: Leonardo da Vinci.

Machiavelli had probably met the fifty-two-year-old Leonardo almost two years earlier, when the itinerant artist was serving as Cesare Borgia's military architect. Though Leonardo was known in Florence principally as a painter, he had long nourished ambitions in the field of military engineering—a fine irony in a vegetarian who despised hunters and could not bear to see a bird in a cage. But when he left Florence for Milan in 1482, aged thirty, Leonardo was armed with a letter to Lodovico Sforza that outlined his expertise in, among other things, constructing catapults and cannons, draining moats, and destroying fortresses with tunnels and bombs (only at the end of this letter did he mention that he was also able to paint and sculpt). He had remained at the Sforza court for the next seventeen years, designing (though not actually building) military hardware such as crossbows, machine guns that would increase the volume and speed of fire, and even a four-wheeled tank armed with cannons and sheathed in metal plate. He also studied ballistics so cannonballs could be aimed more accurately at the enemy. Somehow he managed to find the time amid all these activities to paint *The Last Supper* and invent the world's first toilet seat.

Leonardo seems to have begun work on plans for the Arno diversion as early as the summer of 1503, when he visited locations in the river valley with a musician named Giovanni Piffero, father of the goldsmith Benvenuto Cellini, then an infant. He had then returned to Florence and over the next few months made feasibility studies related to the canal's construction. Among his calculations were studies enabling him to estimate that the task of moving a million tons of earth would consume 54,000 man-days and require various digging machines, for which he produced designs. Nothing would be left to chance. He even computed that each bucket of dirt would pass through the hands of no fewer than fourteen laborers as it ascended from the bottom of the canal to its brink.

The diversion of the Arno was intended to produce beneficial effects for Florence quite apart from the subjugation of the Pisans, since it would make the Arno more navigable and also provide a defense against the flooding that regularly destroyed crops and inundated Florence itself. The project quickly won the support of Piero Soderini, and by the summer of 1504 the Gonfalonier had managed to persuade his colleagues in the Signoria of its desirability. The first spade of dirt was turned on August 20, with 2,000 workmen, protected by another thousand soldiers, earning one carlino a day for their labors in the baking heat. To put this paltry wage into context, one carlino a day was what, in the same month, Leonardo agreed to charge a new apprentice to live and work in his house.

By this time, Leonardo had left the project to return to work with his paintbrush: not only on the *Mona Lisa* but also on a vast mural showing the Battle of Anghiari, a 1440 Florentine victory over Milan, that the Signoria had hired him to paint on a wall in the Hall of the Great Council. Affairs were left at least partly in the hands of Machiavelli, who, from his desk in the Chancellery, began writing dozens of letters on behalf of the Ten to the overseers in the field. Machiavelli probably supported the canal project from the outset. He may even have been part of the group that visited the Arno valley with Leonardo in the summer of 1503. In any case, he and Leonardo had struck up a collaborative relationship soon after their return from Imola. Machiavelli's influence with the government secured Leonardo's mural project in the Palazzo della Signoria. He signed Leonardo's contract with the Signoria in May 1504, and his assistant, Agostino Vespucci, translated into Italian a Latin account of the Battle of Anghiari from which Leonardo (who had no Latin) would work.

While Machiavelli handled the administration, the technical aspects of the canal project were the responsibility of an engineer named Colombino. Based on Leonardo's calculations, Colombino hoped to complete the canal inside of a month; but matters soon went contrary to plan. Impressive though his studies were, Leonardo's calculations proved wildly optimistic, and it rapidly became clear that much more labor would be required. Worse still, there were design flaws that made Brunelleschi's ill-fated dam at Lucca seem a masterstroke of civil engineering.

Machiavelli became aware of problems within a month of work having started. He already entertained doubts about Colombino's leadership qualities and strength of character: "As a person he is so reserved," he informed one of the commissioners, "that he does not stand out among such a multitude of men and preparations." By the middle of September he had reason to question Colombino's engineering expertise as well. The engineer made a number of changes to Leonardo's design, in part because Machiavelli's letters continually stressed the need for haste. Machiavelli became concerned that the canal's gradient was not steep enough and that its bed would be higher than that of the Arno. His worries were well-founded, since by the end of September the water from the Arno was failing to enter the canal except at high tide, and as the tide ebbed the water simply flowed back into the riverbed. Soderini managed to get a reprieve for the project by forcing through the Council of Eighty a decree ordering work to continue, but by then the canal looked increasingly doomed. According to one of the commissioners on the site, the laborers were working "with a bad disposition," while Colombino himself was despairing of success and "laying the blame on unfavorable circumstances." Machiavelli's letters show he was still hoping to rescue the project as late as the first week of October, but at that point the whole undertaking ended abruptly and ingloriously when a violent storm struck, causing the walls of the canal to collapse. The project was speedily abandoned, and the Pisans came out to fill in the ditch. "How great a distance there is," the historian Francesco Guicciardini sighed gloomily, "between planning things and putting them in operation."

In the end, the disastrous enterprise to divert the course of the Arno cost 7,000 ducats and claimed the lives of eighty workmen. It also cost Piero Soderini and his colleagues a good deal of prestige. The immediate consequence of the extravagant failure was a fiscal crisis in Florence, which led in turn to a perilous political situation. Angered by the tax burden caused by the incompetent prosecution of the war by Soderini, the Great Council of the People refused to pass tax legislation proposed by the Signoria. Deprived of tax revenues, Soderini was unable to pay protection money (40,000 ducats per year) to Florence's most crucial ally, Louis XII of France; and without the protection of Louis XII, Florence would be at the mercy of the Spaniards.

The Spanish threat to Florence had become increasingly real in the summer of 1504, as Machiavelli received reports in the Chancellery that Bartolomeo d'Alviano, a *condottiere* in the pay of Gonsalvo de Córdoba, was heading north from Rome with an army of several thousand men "to overthrow our government and bring Tuscany under Spain's control." The conquest of Florence was intended to be the first step in a complex plan by the Spaniards to expel the French from Milan. The French defeat in Naples in 1503 had raised hopes in their enemies that the duchy could be recovered for the Sforza family. Since Florence under Soderini was a staunch French ally, Lodovico Sforza's brother, a cardinal named Ascanio, made arrangements with Gonsalvo de Córdoba whereby the Florentine Republic would be overthrown and the Medici restored to power; the Medici would then assist in the eviction of the French from Milan.

It was in this atmosphere of fear and rumor, in November 1504, that Machiavelli began composing a 550-line poem entitled *Decennale primo* (First Decennium). Taking two weeks to write, the poem is a narrative of "Italian hardships" over the previous ten years. Its unremitting catalogue of horror and pain—Machiavelli's verse pitilessly recounts "happenings cruel and savage"—is relieved at the very end by a breath of optimism suggesting that the Italians can once again seize control of their affairs: they must "reopen the Temple of Mars." With this metaphor he urges the Italians to abandon the feckless and treacherous *condottieri* and rely on themselves instead—specifically, on militias made up of their own citizens. The exhortation was much more than a literary conceit. In the wake of the canal's failure, Machiavelli turned his attention to this project as the salvation not just of Florence, but of all Italy.

Chapter Eight

THE FAILURE OF the Arno project was followed early in 1505 by further humiliation for Florence at the hands of the Pisans. In March, Florentine forces, commanded by a substandard *condottiere* named Lucca Savelli, were given a sound drubbing at Ponte a Capelletto. Fifty of their soldiers were killed by a smaller contingent of Pisans, while 370 were marched into captivity. Survivors of the battle were then set upon and robbed by peasants as they retreated. The defeat prevented grain imports from reaching Florence, causing the price of corn to rise steadily throughout April. Famine and bread riots followed in May.

Seeking a solution to the problem, the Signoria sent Machiavelli fifty miles southeast to Castiglione del Lago, on the western shore of Lake Trasimeno, to negotiate with Gianpaolo Baglioni of Perugia. Baglioni had previously signed a contract to fight on behalf of Florence; by the spring of 1505, however, bribed by Medici supporters and influenced by his brother-in-law, Bartolomeo d'Alviano (who was himself in the midst of preparing an invasion of Florence on behalf of Spain), was trying to wriggle out of his obligations on the pretext that he needed his troops for his own defense. Machiavelli "pricked him right and left," as he reported to the Signoria. There is certainly an element of irony in Machiavelli lecturing someone, as he did to Baglioni, about his "reputation for good faith" and the importance of keeping his word. Baglioni, unswayed by the arguments, held firm in his refusal.

Despite failing at this mission, Machiavelli was invested with full diplomatic powers and delegated to Mantua; here he bargained more successfully with Francesco Gonzaga, the Marquess of Mantua. Florence also reenlisted Ercole Bentivoglio, a member of the ruling family in Bologna. This forty-six-year-old *condottiere* had more than two decades of experience fighting against Venice, Genoa, and Siena. In 1501 he had supported Vitellozzo Vitelli's campaign against Florence, though soon afterward, in one of the swaps of allegiance for which *condottieri* were famous, he led Florentine troops against the Pisans (a campaign from which he was distracted when he accused his wife, Barbara, of adultery, then attempted to poison her).

The signatures of these *condottieri* were secured in the nick of time. In early August an army of some 2,000 men commanded by Alviano, including mounted crossbowmen, poured into Tuscany. Machiavelli's frantic bargaining of the previous few months seemed for naught as the Florentines found themselves ill-served by their allies. As Alviano appeared on the horizon, the French refused any assistance on the grounds, shortsighted in the extreme, that Florence was late in its payment of 40,000 ducats, while the cowardly Marquess of Mantua (who often used his attacks of syphilis to excuse himself from the fray) declined to fight on the pretext that the French had not approved his contract. Fortunately, Ercole Bentivoglio, the man who conquered Ripafratta, was made of sterner stuff. On August 17 he trounced Alviano at San Vincenzo, killing or disarming the entire enemy army and capturing Alviano's baggage-train and a thousand horses. The Florentines, a people unused to celebrating military exploits, put Alviano's standards and helmet triumphantly on display in the hall of the Great Council of the People.

Exhilarated by such an overwhelming victory and determined to press their advantage, Soderini and the Signoria next sent Bentivoglio to assail Pisa. The *condottiere* made an encouraging start in the first week of September, blasting down sections of the city walls with his artillery. In a disheartening reprise of 1499, however, Bentivoglio's troops mutinied against their captains and refused to enter the city. The effort was abandoned, with Florence yet again suffering shame and disrepute.

Machiavelli chose the moment of this inglorious downturn in Florentine fortunes to advance his new scheme. He had become convinced that most of Florence's shame and woe could be laid at the door of the *condottieri*. He had long resented the circumstances by which Florence was compelled to deliver its fortunes into the hands of men who possessed neither loyalty nor integrity beyond what could be purchased for a bag of ducats. He had watched as the Republic was repeatedly thwarted by the treachery of Paolo Vitelli, the indiscipline and cupidity of the Swiss, the double-dealing of Gianpaolo Baglioni, the mediocrity of Lucca Savelli, and now the pusillanimity of the Marquess of Mantua. Florence clearly needed to sever her dependence on these self-interested and unscrupulous soldiers of fortune. But from where, in that case, would her arms and weapons be found?

Among the many things that impressed Machiavelli about Cesare Borgia had been his deployment of a citizen militia made up from the vigorous, hard-bitten peasants of the Romagna. Faced with the loss of his mercenary fighters during the crisis of 1502, Borgia had conscripted bands of warriors with which to face the threat. Reviewing them on parade in Imola, Machiavelli had been inspired by more than just their fetching crimson-and-yellow uniforms: here were men whose incentive to fight was their homeland—the survival of their houses, farms, and families—rather than the prospect of payment or plunder.

Once upon a time, as Machiavelli well knew, Florence, too, had had its own communal militia. In the mid-thirteenth century all young men in the city and surrounding countryside had been enrolled into ninety-five companies. Summoned by the authorities in times of crisis by the tolling of a bell, called the *Martinella*, they were obliged to appear under arms and ready for battle. Various ceremonies and traditions prevailed, one of the strangest of which was the ringing of the *Martinella* for a full month before the enemy was attacked—a ritual indicative of extreme self-confidence, not to mention the belief that taking an enemy by surprise was a shameful tactic. It had soon become clear, however, that citizens in a wealthy mercantile republic did not necessarily make the best soldiers, nor did they serve the state's economic advantage when they embarked on lengthy military campaigns that kept them from their businesses and farms or, worse still, got them killed. One catastrophic encounter with a small group of German knights outside the gates of Siena in 1260, at the Battle of Montaperti, had resulted in 4,000 Florentine casualties, affecting, it was said, men from every family. By the middle of the fourteenth century, the militia had entered a period of decline, and when Florence went to war with Lucca in 1336 it did so only after spending 100,000 florins on foreign mercenaries. A century later, wars in Italy were fought almost exclusively by *condottieri*.

Machiavelli believed that, whatever its drawbacks, the old citizen militia had been responsible for safeguarding Florentine liberties and generating the city's prosperity. As early as the spring of 1504 he had discussed with Francesco Soderini, the Gonfalonier's brother, the idea of reviving the institution. Soderini (recently made a cardinal) encouraged the initiative, calling it "a thing so necessary and so sound." Those in a greater authority had evidently thought otherwise at that point, committing themselves instead to the ill-fated canal. Still, Cardinal Soderini urged Machiavelli to keep the faith: "Do not leave off, for perhaps the favor that is not given one day will be given another."

In the autumn of 1505, the time had come and the favor was given. Machiavelli presently received authorization from the Gonfalonier and the Signoria to begin recruiting a citizen army on a trial basis. The first weeks of 1506 found him at his new headquarters in Poppi, a small hilltop town in the Casentino, twenty-five miles east of Florence. A valley of the upper Arno, the Casentino was a beautiful but forbidding region, with arduous hills crisscrossed by steep mule trails and covered with thick pinewoods where eagles nested and wild boars prowled. It was known for its monasteries and mystics: Saint Francis had received the stigmata on a Casentino mountainside. Yet it was also a region plagued by bandits and thieves, a lawless outback where, as a report from the Signoria grimly stated, "every day armed disputes and homicides occurred." But it was from the sturdy menfolk of this region, and from the neighboring valley of the Mugello to the west, that Machiavelli hoped to forge his militia.

Machiavelli's ambitious aim was to raise no fewer than 10,000 men. To that end, he began enlisting for service all men between the ages of eighteen and thirty. The recruits were to be integrated into some thirty companies, each with three hundred men; several companies from the same valley or a set of neighboring villages would form a battalion under the command of a constable. One man of every ten was to be armed with a musket, while the others would wield pikes, crossbows, or other weapons. The companies were to be exercised on various feast days—but no more, it was decreed, than sixteen times a year—while the battalions would be reviewed by their constables every six months. To appease those (and there were many) who feared the prospect of arming the rabble, discipline was harsh and unforgiving. Desertion was punishable by death, while the failure of a conscript to appear for drills and parades in the local piazza came in for only slightly less rigorous treatment. If these ordinances seemed severe, recruitment may have been assisted by the fact that service in Machiavelli's militia came with an automatic discharge of any outstanding debt or criminal charge.

Machiavelli encountered a number of difficulties assembling his militiamen. For one thing, the weather in the first few weeks of 1506 was so cold that the rivers froze solid, such that games of *calcio*, a violent and primitive version of soccer, were played on the Arno. More seriously, he discovered that the people of the Mugello and Casentino had little patriotic feeling for Florence and therefore no special desire to take up arms in its service. They had, moreover, even less love for each other. This was a region rife with feuds and vendettas: Machiavelli discovered that the villagers of Petrognano despised those in nearby Campana, and vice versa, with such ardor that they refused to serve together in the same battalion. Nor did the feeble financial incentive do much to create enthusiastic recruits. The Signoria, tightfisted as ever, would pay these warriors three ducats per month if a war took them from their homes and farms, while the effort of marching and drilling on feast days brought them no recompense at all.

Nonetheless, Machiavelli managed through his energy and efficiency to assemble enough soldiers to stage a drill in Florence in the middle of February. Four hundred farmers from the Mugello were carted into the city, outfitted in white waistcoats, red-and-white stockings, white caps, and iron breastplates, and then marched with muskets and lances through the Piazza della Signoria. The Florentines were agog at this troop of peasant-warriors. "This was thought the finest thing that had ever been arranged for Florence," wrote one observer. A few weeks later, Cardinal Soderini wrote a letter of congratulation to his friend: "You must get no small satisfaction from the fact that such a worthy thing should have been given its beginnings by your hands. Please persevere and bring it to the desired end."

In April, Machiavelli engaged the infamous Don Michelotto as *bargello*, or chief of police, for his militia. The appointment was logical enough given the Spaniard's instrumental role in organizing and policing Cesare Borgia's Romagnol militia a few years earlier. But the arrival of the most sinister of all Borgia's henchmen caused some disquiet. Condemned by one Florentine as a "monster of iniquity" and an "enemy of God and man," Don Michelotto had left behind a truly horrific trail of violence and murder. His specialty was strangulation, and many others besides Vitellozzo Vitelli and Oliverotto da Fermo had expired in the grip of his rope. His victims included Alfonso of Aragón, second husband of Lucrezia Borgia, as well as the secretary of Pope Alexander VI, Francesco Troche. After Borgia's conquest of Camerino, he had strangled its ruler, Giulio Cesare da Varano, and his three young sons. He had even strangled a shoemaker in Forlì who asked too high a price, in Don Michelotto's opinion, for a pair of boots. When he attacked Fossombrone on behalf of Borgia in October 1502, so appalling was his reputation that, according to legend, many people had committed suicide rather than fall into his clutches.

This, then, was the man on whom rested Machiavelli's dreams for the liberty, security, and prosperity of Florence. Don Michelotto was given orders to ride into the Florentine dominions and pacify them by purging the Casentino of thieves, rebels, and various other troublemakers. Unsurprisingly, he took to the task with gusto, setting off with a force of 150 mercenaries and burning down the houses of suspected bandits. The Signoria was quickly forced to issue commands for him to govern with a gentler hand. Still, his efforts, and more especially those of Machiavelli, seemed to pay satisfactory dividends: by the end of the summer, 500 of his militiamen were fighting in Pisan territory.

Chapter Nine

S OON AFTER COMING to power in 1503, Pope Julius II had won the nickname *Il Papa Terribile*—the "dreadful" or "terrifying" pope. He was indeed a formidable character. "It is almost impossible," wrote a Venetian ambassador, "to describe how strong and violent and difficult to manage he is. In body and soul he has the nature of a giant. Everything about him is on a magnified scale, both his undertakings and passions." The gargantuan scale of Julius's ambitions was reflected in such projects as the rebuilding of the basilica of St. Peter's (the foundation stone for which he had laid during Holy Week in 1506) and the commissioning of Michelangelo to carve his tomb: a fifty-foot-high monument that was to include forty life-size marble figures.

Julius had equally grandiose plans for strengthening the prestige and authority of the Church. One of his first acts after entering the Vatican had been to promulgate a bull declaring the inalienable rights of the Church over the usurpers of her domains. He had particularly in mind the Romagna, as well as the cities of Bologna and Perugia. Within two years, thanks to reducing his household expenses and selling various positions within the Church, he had amassed a prodigious war chest of some 400,000 ducats, with which he was determined to buy troops for a major military enterprise. With some of these funds he hoped to purchase the services of the twenty-eight-year-old *condottiere* Marcantonio Colonna, a hero of the Battle of Garigliano who had just married Julius's niece, Lucrezià. There was one minor drawback: Colonna was already under contract to the Republic of Florence. The Signoria was reluctant to dispense with his services because he was assisting in the interminable campaign against Pisa, and so in the summer of 1506 they decided to send an emissary to Rome to rebuff the pope and play for time. Niccolò Machiavelli was forced to interrupt work on his militia and travel to the court of *Il Papa Terribile*.

As it happened, Julius departed from Rome for his military adventure at exactly the same time Machiavelli left Florence. On August 17 the pope announced that he intended to lead his army in person against the vicars of the Romagna. "Certainly the pope must have had too much wine!" exclaimed Louis XII. But Julius was as good as his word. On August 26 he left Rome with 500 men-at-arms and several thousand Swiss pikemen. Also along for the campaign were twenty-six cardinals, much of the Vatican bureaucracy, the architect Donato Bramante, and the choir of the Sistine Chapel. At the head of the procession was the consecrated Host, which had been imprinted with scenes from the Crucifixion and Resurrection. Machiavelli joined this bizarre expedition at Nepi, twenty miles north of Rome, and then, with growing incredulity, watched events unfold.

"No one believes," Machiavelli reported to the Signoria, "that the pope will be able to achieve his ends." Yet Julius would repeatedly defy the predictions of the skeptics. His first objective was Perugia, the Umbrian city ruled by the Baglioni family. It was a city steeped in treachery and bloodshed. Six years earlier the Baglioni had hosted the outrage known as the "Scarlet Wedding," when twenty-five-year-old Grifonetto Baglioni and his supporters massacred members of their own family following a two-week-long wedding celebration. The young bridegroom, Astore Baglioni, was murdered and had his heart eaten by his kinsman Filippo Baglioni. Grifonetto was soon afterward butchered in the street by Gianpaolo Baglioni, who had already murdered his own father and taken his sister as his mistress. Gianpaolo proved more temperate, though, in his dealings with the pope. Meeting with Julius at Orvieto early in September, he acceded to all of his demands, agreeably handing over fortresses and hostages. Julius and his cardinals then made their way to Perugia, which they entered, unarmed, on September 13.

Machiavelli had met the loathsome Gianpaolo in 1505. Now he watched with gruesome fascination as Julius placed himself at the mercy of this treacherous and well-armed tyrant. He was amazed at the pope's apparent foolhardiness, and at what he later called Baglioni's cowardice. He had clearly been expecting—and even hoping—to witness a Borgia-like deception, a display of force and fraud that would conclude with the slaying of Julius. He believed, as he later wrote, that Baglioni had a "perfect opportunity" to kill the pope. The execution of Julius would have been "a deed for which everyone would have admired his courage and for which he would have left an everlasting remembrance of himself." The "greatness" of the deed, he argued, would have outweighed any accusations of infamy. Yet despite his numerous acts of perfidy, Gianpaolo Baglioni balked at the thought of killing a pope.[1]

Machiavelli's literary sanction of the murder of a pope was written long after the event, at a time when he believed he had just cause to abominate Julius, whom he claimed (with hypocritical horror) was "bent on the ruin of Christianity." In the immediate aftermath of the event, however, he had turned his attention not to apologize for committing murder in the name of justice, but rather to a political conundrum. Close-up observation of Julius had obviously set him to thinking about the elements of political leadership. In 1503 he had been troubled by the downfall of Cesare Borgia, who seemed to have done everything right. Now he was puzzled by the success of the pope, who seemed to have done everything wrong. What lessons, if any, could be taken from these unexpected developments?

While still in Perugia, Machiavelli composed a long letter to Giovan Battista Soderini, the twenty-two-year-old son of the Gonfalonier. The letter took the form of an extended meditation—some 1,200 words' worth—on what he called "the action of men and their ways of doing things." History showed, he wrote, that divergent courses of action could bring about similar ends, while comparable ways of proceeding often produced widely varying results. Lorenzo the Magnificent, for example, had disarmed the people of Florence in order to maintain his position, while in Bologna, by contrast, Giovanni Bentivoglio had accomplished precisely the same end by arming the populace. Foremost in Machiavelli's mind, though, were the actions of Julius II, "who has no scales or measuring stick in his house," yet who obtained through impetuosity "what ought to have been difficult to attain even with organization and with weapons."

Machiavelli claimed to be at a loss to explain these variations between action and outcome. "The reason why different actions are sometimes equally useful and sometimes equally detrimental I do not know," he confessed to Giovan Battista, "yet I should very much like to." He then proceeded to tender the young man his own opinion. "I believe that just as Nature has created men with different faces," he wrote, "so she has created them with different intellects and imaginations. As a result, each man behaves according to his own intellect and imagination." One man is naturally cruel, that is, while another is naturally compassionate; others are impetuous by nature, still others cautious or calculating. The man whose natural abilities match the temper of the times will obviously be successful, while anyone who proves incapable of this assimilation will inevitably fail. "And truly, anyone wise enough to adapt to and understand the times and the pattern of events," Machiavelli wrote, "would always have good fortune or would always keep himself from bad fortune."

If at this point Giovan Battista had been expecting a disquisition on how best to understand the pattern of events and thereby adapt to the times, he would have been sorely disappointed. Machiavelli did not seek to explain the contrasting behavior of Lorenzo the Magnificent and Giovanni Bentivoglio with a study of, say, the social and political differences between Florence and Bologna: he merely attributed particular patterns of behavior to men's distinctive and inescapable natures. "Men are unable to master their own natures," he wrote, and therefore they must always act in the way prescribed by their characters. Far from being able to adapt their behavior to events, they can change "neither their imaginations nor their ways of doing things." Men were utterly powerless, Machiavelli told Giovan Battista, to take stock of the times and then to shape their actions accordingly. An impetuous leader such as Julius II could only ever act with impetuosity. He would be successful so long as—by some fortunate coincidence—the times called for impulsive, headlong action; but defeat would be the outcome as soon as caution and constraint were required.

This bleakly deterministic view seems to have been carried over from Machiavelli's earlier correspondence with Bartolomeo Vespucci regarding the influence of the stars. Then, Vespucci had assured him that the wise man had the power to select or alter his course of action, "changing his own step, now one way and now another." Two years later, Machiavelli rejected this idea: if men could indeed adopt the appropriate course of action, "it would come to be true that the wise man could control the stars and the Fates. But such wise men do not exist," he concluded pessimistically in his letter to Giovan Battista. The constraints of man's nature were such that no variations or corrective steps were possible.

Giovan Battista may well have reacted to these propositions with surprise and disbelief. Not only did Machiavelli's view of man differ from that of astrologers such as Vespucci; it was likewise sharply at odds with most theological and philosophical thinking of the time. Aquinas was only one of many writers who believed wise men capable of using reason to resist their natural inclinations. Machiavelli's view of man was most spectacularly at odds, though, with the one eloquently expressed in Giovanni Pico della Mirandola's *Oration on the Dignity of Man*, first printed in 1486. Pico argued that man was the most miraculous product of Creation because, unlike other creatures, he was utterly unconstrained by the laws of nature. God gave man the freedom and ability to trace for himself the contours of his own nature. "Oh wonderous and unsurpassable felicity of man!" Pico exclaimed, "to whom it is granted to have what he chooses, to be what he wills to be."[2] Machiavelli, though, forcefully denied man this exhilarating freedom, placing him instead in a prison-house of necessity and permitting him to act only according to the dictates of his nature.

This grim and even cynical philosophy is far less appealing than Pico's, but it is one to which Machiavelli would return whenever he contemplated "the action of men and their ways of doing things." Not merely the transitory consequence of his bafflement at Julius's unaccountable success in Perugia in 1506, his view of the implacability of human nature will reappear, years later, in a number of his most famous writings.

The military expedition of Julius II did not end in Perugia. After a week in the city, the pope and his entourage departed for Bologna, another rebel fiefdom that he wished to take back into the control of the Church. Giovanni Bentivoglio anxiously consulted a young astrologer, Luca Gaurico, to discover what manner of fate awaited him. When the stars failed to augur well, Bentivoglio subjected Gaurico to the *mancuerda*, a method of torture in which a cord was tightened around the victim's arms by means of a lever until it sliced through to the bone. When the stars still portended no good despite these coercions, Bentivoglio and his sons bowed to the inevitable: they abandoned the city and fled to Milan. Julius and his army arrived to take possession of Bologna, amid wild celebrations, on November 10. *Il Papa Terribile* at once gained a new nickname: the "Warrior Pope."

Machiavelli was back in Florence by this time, having spent almost two months at the papal court. He may have returned with some apprehension for both the survival of his militia project and his position in the Chancellery. Early in October he had received a letter from Biagio Buonaccorsi reporting that he had been condemned as a "rascal" by Alamanno Salviati, the man to whom he had dedicated the *First Decennium*. "I never entrusted anything at all to that rascal since I have been one of the Ten," Salviati had supposedly remarked before "going on in this vein or better." The exact word Salviati had used was *ribaldo*, which means scoundrel or wretch but also has the connotation of a humble birth, since a *ribaldo* was literally a lowly footsoldier: a scathing reference, perhaps, to Machiavelli's modest social origins.

A member of a wealthy family of Florentine bankers, Salviati was one of the foremost members of a group of patricians known as the *ottimati*. (This epithet, from the Latin *optimates*, "best ones," alluded to an aristocratic faction during the late Roman Republic.) Well-heeled and socially prominent *ottimati* like Salviati believed that the Great Council of the People had transferred power from their hands into those of an inferior class of citizens. In 1502 Salviati and his friends had supported Piero Soderini (who came from a rich and venerable family like their own) in hopes that as Gonfalonier for Life he would represent their interests and give them more conspicuous and influential roles in government. By 1506 these hopes had largely been betrayed, and Salviati and a number of other *ottimati* turned against the Gonfalonier. Machiavelli became embroiled in this factional discord because he was seen by the *ottimati*—quite correctly—as a friend and ally of Soderini. A number of *ottimati* even began referring to him as the Gonfalonier's *mannerino*, or puppet.

Despite the factionalism, opposition to Machiavelli's militia project had evidently weakened over the previous year. Not only was he reconfirmed as Second Chancellor, but on December 6, following a vote of 841–317 in the Great Council, he was appointed Secretary of a new magistracy known as the

Nine Officials of the Florentine Ordnance and Militia. This magistracy was given the job of raising a force of 10,000 militiamen and equipping them with firearms, lances, and iron breastplates. Machiavelli was soon back in the hills and valleys, mustering hardy warriors for the enterprise that Cardinal Soderini praised as "a God-given thing."

Chapter Ten

I N T H E S P R I N G of 1507, just when the Spanish threat in Italy seemed to have eased, another foreign aggressor loomed on the horizon. Maximilian I of Habsburg had been head of the Holy Roman Empire since 1493. The Holy Roman Empire consisted of an enormous agglomeration of lands in Central Europe that members of the Habsburg dynasty had ruled, off and on, since 1273. As Voltaire would later observe, it was neither holy, nor Roman, nor an empire. If it had a founding moment, then it was on Christmas Day in the year 800, when Charlemagne was crowned *Imperator Augustus* by Pope Leo III in the basilica of St. Peter's in Rome. In keeping with this tradition, all Holy Roman Emperors had received their crowns from the pope. Maximilian's father had been crowned in Rome by Pope Nicholas V in 1452, and though Frederick died in 1493, Maximilian had yet to make his way from Innsbruck to Rome for his own coronation. In 1507, however, he finally began preparations for a belated journey into Italy.

Word of Maximilian's plans caused alarm in both France and Italy. The trip to Rome would require him to cross through Lombardy, and King Louis XII feared, with good reason, that as the husband of Bianca Maria Sforza, the daughter of Galeazzo Maria, Maximilian was using the coronation as a pretext to enter Italy and oust the French from Milan. The Florentines, as France's ally, found themselves at risk of becoming embroiled in a war much larger than their contest with Pisa. The Signoria resolved that an envoy should be sent to the imperial court to gauge Maximilian's capabilities and intentions. Thanks to the influence of Piero Soderini, Machiavelli was given the task on June 19, but little more than a week later his appointment was rescinded at the behest of the *ottimati*, who favored one of their own in place of Soderini's churlish *mannerino*. The assignment went instead to a young blueblood named Francesco Vettori.

Machiavelli was so deeply resentful of this slight that a friend was still condoling with him a month later. But at least the revocation allowed him to spend much of the summer mobilizing his militia. Eighteen months after his first expedition to the Casentino, much work remained to be done. Though Don Michelotto assured him the battalions were "without disorder and with admirable discipline," reports to the contrary had begun reaching Florence. Wine had been stolen from a vineyard, and on another occasion a dozen drunken militiamen caused such affront in a tavern that the ringleader was tortured on orders of the Ten of Liberty and Peace and then tossed into prison. Various militiamen had also gone absent without leave ("I shall plunge this sword into his heart," declared Don Michelotto of one straying crossbowman). Worst of all, reports had begun arriving of Don Michelotto's own disorder and indiscipline, including an armed struggle at a house in Castrocaro. "I shall stand and be judged before God," a self-righteous Don Michelotto wrote to Machiavelli in defense of his actions. But Machiavelli immediately began looking for a replacement for his depraved and reviled *bargello*. Don Michelotto would be dismissed a few months later; and a few months after that, in an act that few could have mourned, he was killed by an anonymous assailant during a skirmish in Milan.

Another opportunity to travel to the court of Maximilian eventually presented itself in December as Soderini persuaded his colleagues in the Signoria that a second representative was needed besides Vettori, a rather lazy and feckless young man whose reports did little to enlighten. Machiavelli set off in the middle of December for Bolzano, the Tyrolean city where Maximilian's court was residing. Despite the poor roads and bad weather he chose a meandering route via Geneva (which added hundreds of miles to his journey) and Constance. Curious about the Swiss, whose infantry (notwithstanding their disgraceful behavior at Pisa) was the best in Europe, he turned the expedition into a fact-finding mission. He spent four days among the Swiss, observing "how they lived and what sort of people they were." If Switzerland was business, then Constance was pleasure. Here he took time to visit the Flemish composer Heinrich Isaac, whom he knew from the court of Lorenzo the

Magnificent, where Isaac had been Lorenzo's organist and choirmaster. Music was one of the few arts for which Machiavelli showed any great appreciation, though as a composer of bawdy verses he may have enjoyed Isaac's *canti carnascialeschi*—songs composed for the open air of the piazzas during Carnival—more than his masses and motets.

Machiavelli finally arrived in Bolzano in the second week of January. Since the Florentines were convinced an invasion was imminent, Machiavelli and Vettori were instructed to pursue what might be called cashbox diplomacy: offering Maximilian large sums of money in return for his promise to respect their borders and possessions. They were authorized to offer as much as 50,000 ducats, but only if they could be absolutely certain he was indeed going to invade. Maximilian's intentions were difficult to establish, especially since the forty-eight-year-old ruler hardly seemed to know them himself. Machiavelli was singularly unimpressed by this man whose personal emblem was a pomegranate. He struck Machiavelli, by comparison to Cesare Borgia or Julius II, as an extremely indecisive and incompetent ruler. Maximilian, he reported back to the Signoria, was someone who "blows with the wind of every different opinion."

Maximilian proved his worthlessness soon enough. In February, impatient with their refusal to allow his troops to cross their territories, he attacked the Venetians near Vicenza. The Venetians, under the command of Bartolomeo d'Alviano, swiftly defeated his forces and even conquered some of his territories. In June, thus humiliated, Maximilian put his signature to a three-year truce. The threat from the north had been extinguished with astonishing ease. It would take a later emperor, considerably more vigorous and ambitious than Maximilian, to wreak havoc in Italy.

Machiavelli returned to Florence in the middle of June 1508 and, despite a painful attack of gallstones, resumed work on his militia almost immediately. That summer his battalions were given the task of participating in the annual *guasto* (from *guastare*, "to spoil") in the Pisan countryside, helping pickax-wielding peasants lay waste to the fields and vineyards. Their efforts were to be unstinting and merciless. "Press for it to be finished in such a way that the least possible fodder is left to the enemy," Piero Soderini urged him in August.

Besides destroying their crops, the Florentines were hoping to starve the Pisans into submission by blockading the city. The new plan was somewhat simpler than Leonardo's doomed canal project. A barrier was constructed downstream from Pisa at San Pietro in Grado (the spot where legend claimed Saint Peter had first alighted in Italy) to prevent foodstuffs and other supplies reaching the city from the coast. When the Pisans got around the blockade by means of a canal named the Fiume Morto, or "Dead River," the architect Antonio da Sangallo the Elder was hired to build a wooden dam across it. Machiavelli and his militiamen were then entrusted with protecting these two obstructions from enemy attack. "We have placed on your shoulders the responsibility for all this," the Ten reminded him. February 1509 thus found Machiavelli leading a thousand troops to the mouth of the Fiume Morto and placing himself in such personal jeopardy that the members of the Ten became perturbed, urging him to move to the safer environs of the Florentine camp at Cascina. "I know the camp would be less dangerous and less arduous," Machiavelli wrote back to them, "but had I not wanted danger and hard work, I would not have left Florence."

Machiavelli's brave actions in the field were causing disquiet elsewhere, though for a quite different reason. The commissioner in charge of overseeing the campaign against Pisa, Niccolò Capponi, was displeased with his lack of reports from the Second Chancellor. At the end of February, a worried Biagio informed Machiavelli that Capponi was "grumbling and complaining that you have never written to him." The thirty-five-year-old Capponi, a member of one of the grandest of all Florentine families, may have been motivated by the entrenched *ottimati* antagonism to Soderini and Machiavelli. Even so, Biagio could not understand why his superior, so wise in other ways, seemed either not to know how to conciliate his enemies or else not to comprehend the necessity of doing so. "The more powerful must be right," he wrote pointedly to Machiavelli, "and one must show respect for them. So you have to get used to being patient and knowing how to behave on such occasions. . . . So if one or two letters are needed to make him happy, it will not take much effort." But, as in the case of Agnolo Tucci, the disgruntled paper merchant, Machiavelli showed himself unwilling or unable to use compliments and blandishments to disarm his enemies; he was simply unable to flatter to deceive. "Men," as he himself had written, "are unable to master their own natures."

The lesson Machiavelli took away from his dispute with Capponi was that (as Piero Soderini wrote to him placatingly) "the way of this world is to receive great ingratitude for great and good operations." Soderini wrote these words at the end of February. Within a few months, however, the blockade began to take its devastating effect. Machiavelli was forced to reduce the numbers of his militia by a third as the season approached when many of his soldiers had to put down their weapons and start toiling in the fields. Nonetheless, only the smallest amounts of grain made it through the blockade, and by the spring many in Pisa were dying of starvation. Bowing at last to the inevitable, the Pisans sent a delegation to Florence and signed a treaty of surrender at the beginning of June, bringing to an end almost fifteen years of warfare.

Machiavelli was present for the ceremony in the Palazzo della Signoria, putting his name next to that of Adriani, the First Chancellor. As the document was being signed, a dove came through the window and flew over the heads of the Ten. The dove then crashed into a wall and fell dead at the feet of the Ten, but its appearance was still considered a good omen. "Although many said there was nothing supernatural about it," reported a contemporary of Machiavelli, "nevertheless it was a great thing that the dove should have gone to the Ten, who had just made the agreement. . . . Religious men say it came from God."

Whether they came from God or elsewhere, such omens were held in high repute by many Florentines. Doves were a particularly evocative portent, since one of them, of the artificial variety, prefigured the fortunes of Florence in an annual ritual. Every Easter Sunday, a mechanical dove was released along a wire stretched above the congregation in the cathedral of Santa Maria del Fiore. Lit from a flame kindled from chips of stone taken from the Holy Sepulchre in Jerusalem, this winged contraption was supposed to ignite a chariot of fireworks at the other end of the wire. If the dove performed the feat and exploded the fireworks, then a good harvest lay in store, while hard times beckoned if the bird miscarried in its flight.

Such omens were everywhere to be found in Florence, especially in times of crisis. It was widely believed that the death of Lorenzo the Magnificent had been foretold by a bolt of lightning that struck the lantern on Brunelleschi's magnificent cupola, sending marble cascading into the street. On that same day, April 5, 1492, two lions kept in an enclosure behind the Palazzo della Signoria—symbols of the Republic's liberty whose behavior was anxiously scrutinized for clues as to the fortunes of the city—fought so frenziedly that both were killed. "I am a dead man!" Lorenzo had exclaimed after learning of these events. Sure enough, he died three days later. Charles VIII's invasion of Italy in 1494 had likewise been presaged by what one chronicler, a friend of Machiavelli's named Francesco Guicciardini, called "celestial signs": three suns had appeared in the sky in Puglia; statues and other sacred images "sweated openly"; and women began giving birth to human monsters. People were only surprised, Guicciardini reported, that no comets had appeared—"an unfailing messenger of the mutation of kingdoms and states."

What did Machiavelli make of portents such as lightning and comets? This sardonic observer of human nature was quite prepared to believe, like so many others, that it was possible to divine the future by means of auguries. His lucid observation of historical events was often fused with credulous fancies. Years later he would write that "nothing important ever happens in a city or in a region that has not been foretold either by diviners or by revelations or by prodigies or by other celestial signs." He confessed not to understand why such revelations should occur, but it may be, he suggested, that "the air about us is full of intelligences." Taking pity on men, these spirits helpfully warn them about upcoming disasters with lightning, comets, and monstrous births.[1]

In keeping with this faith in intelligent spirits and celestial signs, in June 1509 Machiavelli consulted an astrologer in order to determine the best moment for the Florentine commissioners to enter Pisa. Lattanzio Tedaldi, a student and friend of Marsilio Ficino, specialized in interpreting comets and performing astronomical calculations. His reply was helpfully precise. After consulting the heavens, he informed Machiavelli that the commissioners "should on no account enter before six-thirty in the morning, but if it is possible they should enter very shortly after seven o'clock, which will be a very auspicious hour for us." Machiavelli passed along this information, and the commissioners entered Pisa at the prescribed hour on June 8, with the Second Chancellor and selected members of his militia marching alongside. A few hours later, a horseman arrived in Florence bearing an olive branch. Wild celebrations ensued. All shops were closed, bonfires were lit, and the sound of a 17,000-pound bell in the tower of the Palazzo della Signoria, *La Campana del Leone*, "The Lion's Bell," boomed mightily overhead. So general was the rejoicing that even some of the convents bought gunpowder and ignited rockets. As Agostino Vespucci observed, "every man has gone mad with exultation."

If Machiavelli's "great and good operations" had met with thanklessness only a few months earlier, the surrender of Pisa saw him showered with lavish and exuberant gratitude. He received a large share of credit for his work with the militia, with one of the Florentine military commissioners, Filippo Casavecchia, writing to him that his efforts were "to a very great extent" the cause of the victory. Casavecchia then invited Machiavelli to his estate in the country: "I am saving you a ditch full of trout and a wine like you have never drunk." Even Alamanno Salviati had softened his opinion, writing an amicable letter to "my dearest Niccolò" and tendering his fond regards. It was the moment of Machiavelli's greatest triumph. Yet even now the warning signs, for those who chose to see them, were writing themselves across the sky.

Chapter Eleven

Aᴄᴄᴏʀᴅɪɴɢ ᴛᴏ Fʀᴀɴᴄᴇsᴄᴏ Guicciardini, the year 1509 marked the beginning of a dark chapter in Italian history. "There followed throughout Italy, and against the Italians themselves," he wrote, "the cruellest accidents, endless murders, sackings and destruction of many cities and towns, military licentiousness no less pernicious to their friends than to their enemies, religion violated, and holy things trampled under foot." Guicciardini had no doubt about where to point the finger of blame: "These troubles originated from the rash and overly insolent actions of the Venetian Senate."

By 1509 the Venetians had made themselves extremely powerful enemies, both in Italy and abroad. In 1503 they had capitalized on the wreck of Cesare Borgia's fortunes to capture a dozen fortresses in the Romagna, together with Ravenna, Faenza, and Rimini, all of which Pope Julius II regarded as the rightful property of the Holy See. The fortresses had since been returned, but the Venetians declined to surrender their other spoils. "I will never rest," Julius raged at a Venetian envoy, "until you are brought down to be the poor fishermen that you once were."[1]

An opportunity to humble the Venetians had come soon after their defeat of Maximilian's forces in 1508. Though he signed a truce with Venice, Maximilian had immediately set about plotting against the Republic with Louis XII of France, who wished to retrieve cities such as Cremona and Bergamo for the duchy of Milan. On December 10, 1508, their representatives, along with those from the pope and Ferdinand of Aragón, formed the League of Cambrai. According to the treaty's secret clauses, war against Venice was to begin in the spring. The French showed commendable punctuality in sending a 30,000-man army into Italy in the middle of April. Little more than a fortnight later, on May 14, they overwhelmingly defeated the Venetian forces at Agnadello, which lies between Milan and Bergamo. The cities specified in the League of Cambrai swiftly fell into the hands of Venice's enemies as, almost overnight, the Republic lost its purchase on the Italian mainland. The mighty Venetians had indeed been reduced to "poor fishermen."

The Florentines had not been signatories to the League of Cambrai. Instead, pursuing their usual brand of cashbox diplomacy, they agreed to pay 50,000 ducats in two instalments to Louis XII and 40,000 ducats in four instalments to Maximilian. In November 1509, Machiavelli was sent to Mantua, ninety miles north, with one of the disbursements for Maximilian, along with instructions from the Ten to observe the emperor's military strength and gauge his intentions. A few weeks later he moved to Verona, over which Maximilian had asserted his hereditary rights, to gather further information. Good intelligence proved in short supply. "I am high and dry here because we know nothing about anything," he wrote to Luigi Guicciardini, Francesco's older brother and a member of a noble Florentine family. "Still, in order to show signs of life, I dream up diatribes that I write to the Ten."

Such signs of life were necessary. "If ever you were diligent in your reports," Machiavelli had recently been warned by Biagio, "you need to be so now in order to shut the mouths of the *pancacce*." *Pancacce* (from *panca*, "bench" or "seat") was a reference to Machiavelli's armchair critics, the *ottimati* and other malcontents. The expression undoubtedly alludes to the district and corporate representatives who sat on *panche* in the Palazzo della Signoria and spoke for their different rows of benches. But it probably also refers to a wider group of grumblers in Florence's piazzas. Many wealthy merchants constructed wooden benches facing the piazza in front of their shops so they might sit alfresco at closing time, socializing, debating, and gossiping. Biagio's mention of the *pancacce* seems to indicate that Machiavelli's conduct was the subject of these impromptu discussions. Despite the success of the militia, these critics appeared more determined than ever to bring down Soderini's *mannerino*. "Your adversaries are numerous and will stop at nothing," Biagio informed him in December as, taking advantage of Machiavelli's absence from Florence, they launched an anonymous campaign against him.

The first shot was fired in the week before Christmas, when a masked man appeared before a notary to make a statement that Machiavelli was ineligible for office because of (and here Biagio, anxiously reporting the plot, was annoyingly vague) matters related to his late father. Bernardo's transgression may have been illegitimacy, though more likely it was of a financial nature: had Bernardo died owing taxes to the government, for example, then his son's eligibility for public office would be open to question. Biagio claimed the law was on Machiavelli's side, but nonetheless it "was being stretched in a thousand ways and given sinister interpretations by those seeking to act against you."

Machiavelli's predicament was the talk of Florence in the last weeks of 1509, a kind of political scandal that Biagio claimed was spoken of "everywhere, even in the whorehouses." Biagio urged the greatest caution, stating that the "nature of the times" and the fact that many people had "arisen to gossip about this matter and to shout about it everywhere" meant "a good deal of help and scrupulous care" was required. Machiavelli once more had occasion to reflect ruefully on how his tireless operations were rewarded with miserable ingratitude, and Biagio on how his friend seemed constitutionally unable to placate his enemies.

Even as the plot against him was gathering momentum in Florence, Machiavelli managed to steal some lighter moments in Verona. He wrote a letter to Luigi Guicciardini on his favorite philosophical conundrum: "how Fortune hands out to mankind different results under similar circumstances." This time his letter did not expatiate learnedly on political means and ends but dealt, rather, with sexual gratification and revulsion.

Guicciardini had written Machiavelli a letter explaining how (in Machiavelli's delicate paraphrase) "you had hardly finished fucking your woman before you wanted another fuck." Machiavelli then proceeded to tell Guicciardini how similar circumstances had produced, in his case, quite contrary results. What followed was a bawdy and scarcely credible tale of how his laundry woman in Verona (an "old slut") had led him into her house on the pretext of showing him some fine shirts that he might wish to buy. Instead of shirts, though, she offered him a different sort of merchandise: a woman "cowering in a corner affecting modesty with a towel half over her head and face." Left alone in a darkened room with the mysterious woman, "hopelessly horny, I went to her with it," he reported. "Once I had done it, and feeling like taking a look at the merchandise, I took a piece of burning wood from the hearth in the room and lit a lamp that was above it."

Guicciardini must have spotted the punch line to this crude joke long before it emerged in Machiavelli's exquisite humanist script. The lamp revealed, of course, that the woman was monstrously ugly: gray-haired and balding, covered in lice and nits, with rheumy eyes and a twisted, slobbering, toothless mouth. "She exuded such a stench on her breath," he wrote, "that my eyes and nose—twin portals to the most delicate of the senses—felt assaulted by this stench and my stomach became so indignant that it was unable to tolerate this outrage." The encounter concluded with Machiavelli vomiting over the unfortunate creature before making his hasty withdrawal.

One glimpses in this ignoble anecdote the "Machia" who thrilled and amused friends with his ribald tales and impious wit. The story really owes as much to the library or bookshop as it does to the brothel, since it has precedents in the comic stories of wanton women, old procuresses, grotesque bodies, and cruel tricks found in much medieval satire as well as in Giovanni Boccaccio's *Decameron*. It is also part of a long tradition of misogynistic literature running from the invective of Juvenal's *Satires* to Boccaccio's *Corbaccio* and beyond, to works such as Jonathan Swift's "The Lady's Dressing Room," a poem in which the male sexual urge is defeated by the stenches and other attendant horrors of the unadorned female body. Beyond the obscenity and sheer unpleasantness of the tale, though, one can see Machiavelli's inventive mind casually experimenting with ideas that, in days of greater leisure, he would transform into literary productions of a more laudable and durable variety.

The letter to Guicciardini ended on a curious note. Machiavelli informed his friend that once he returned to Florence he hoped to set aside some money and invest in a small business. "I thought about going in for raising chickens," he wrote. The image of Machiavelli raising flocks of chickens must have given Guicciardini almost as much amusement as the tale of the ugly woman of Verona.

The League of Cambrai fell apart early in 1510 as Julius II, leery of an increasing French dominance in Italy, made peace with Venice. In March he concluded a five-year treaty with the Swiss cantons, which agreed to provide him with 6,000 soldiers to protect the interests of the Holy See. His loins thus girded, the Warrior Pope adopted a vehement battle slogan: *Fuori i barbari* ("Out with the barbarians"). By barbarians he meant anyone who was not Italian, but more specifically anyone who was French. By spring it was clear that a large-scale military campaign—one involving the Venetians, the Swiss, and the Church—would soon be launched against Louis XII.

These impending hostilities placed the Florentines, as so often, in a delicate position. Piero Soderini's policies and sentiments were decidedly pro-French, yet the Gonfalonier was extremely reluctant to make an enemy of the pope. The Florentines accordingly elected to assume their usual position on the fence. At the end of June, in hopes of justifying their equivocations, they sent Machiavelli to the court of Louis XII. The Second Chancellor was also urged by Cardinal Soderini "to make every effort to keep that prince [Louis XII] in good union with His Holiness the Pope." It was a momentous and seemingly impossible task.

The times were propitious for Machiavelli to leave Florence. Since returning from Verona in early January he had been recruiting militia around San Miniato, in truffle country midway between Florence and Pisa, and farther north in the Valdinievole. The smear campaign was continuing, though, and in May an anonymous accusation against him reached the Eight of the Watch. This accusation was probably deposited in one of the receptacles known as *tamburi* ("drums") or *buchi della verità* ("holes of truth") that were placed at convenient locations throughout the city, including on the south-facing outside wall of the Palazzo della Signoria. Machiavelli's friend Leonardo da Vinci had fallen victim to one of these denunciations, called *tamburazioni*, in 1476, when he was accused of sodomizing a seventeen-year-old boy. The accusation against Machiavelli was in a similar vein. Into one of these "holes of truth" went a statement reading: "Lords of the Eight, you are hereby informed that Niccolò, son of Bernardo Machiavelli, screws Lucretia, known as La Riccia, in the ass. Interrogate her, and you will learn the truth."

Prostitution was legal in Florence—the municipal brothel could be found only a stone's throw from the cathedral—but sodomy was not. Florence was so notorious for this "abominable vice," as Savonarola had called it, that the German slang term for sodomite was *Florenzer*. Between 1432 and 1502 a special authority had been established to identify and prosecute sodomites (the vast majority for offenses committed with boys rather than women). Called the *Ufficiali di Notte e Conservatori dei Monasteri*, or Officials of the Night and Conservators of Morality in the Monasteries, it had prosecuted more than ten thousand men in its seventy years of operation. Punishments varied according to the record of the offender. A fine was the usual penalty, but during Savonarola's heyday a first-time offender could expect to be punished *alla gogna*, that is, he was tethered to the outer wall of the prison of the Bargello, hands and feet bound, with his hat on the ground to receive money (and rebukes) from passersby and a placard placed around his neck describing his crime. A second offense witnessed the victim tethered to a pillar; a third would get him burned at the stake—though only one sodomite was ever actually executed during the Savonarola years.[2]

Guilty of sodomy or not, Machiavelli certainly knew La Riccia ("Curly"). She may have been the prostitute near the Ponte alle Grazie who waited for him with "open figs" after his first trip to France. In any event, he would be in regular contact with her for at least another decade, an intimacy suggesting that La Riccia herself was not responsible for the accusation. This *tamburazione* was simply another effort by Machiavelli's enemies to blacken his name and thereby undermine his position in the Chancellery. Nothing came of the accusation, but one suspects the scandal brought forth more gossips to "shout about it everywhere." One suspects also that Machiavelli's jaunts to the brothel were not quite what Biagio had in mind when he advised his beleaguered friend that scrupulous care was required to combat his enemies.

The scandal-plagued Second Chancellor departed for France at the end of June, reaching Lyons on July 7. The formidable Roano had died six weeks earlier, but negotiations were no less awkward and difficult for that. Louis XII received Machiavelli soon after his arrival, demanding to know what the Florentine response would be if, as seemed inevitable, French territories in Italy were invaded by the papal armies. Machiavelli managed the usual rhetorical parries, but his reports to the Ten made clear the gravity of a situation whereby they would soon have to declare for either the pope or the king. From a Florentine point of view, war between these two powers would be, he declared, "the most terrifying misfortune that could arise."

Machiavelli finally returned to Florence in October, though not before displaying his contempt for his enemies and their scandal-mongering by revelling in the companionship of a French courtesan by the name of Jeanne. And waiting for him in Florence, it seems, was none other than a certain curly-headed prostitute: "On your arrival there," Roberto Acciaiuoli, the Florentine ambassador to France, wrote to him with a jocular familiarity, "you will perhaps have seen La Riccia again?" Machiavelli was showing as little care as ever for the opinions of his enemies.

Chapter Twelve

THE YEAR 1511 began with heavy snowfalls across Italy. In Florence, city of so many great artists, an enormous snow-lion appeared by the campanile of Santa Maria del Fiore, while the sculptors in the Canto de' Pazzi carved beautiful nudes from blocks of ice. In keeping with the martial spirit of the times, well-fortified snow-castles and fully rigged snow-galleys rose from streets all over the city.[1]

Machiavelli was building castles of his own. He had recently become involved—perhaps due to the influence of his friend Leonardo—in the art and science of military fortification. The liberty of Florence would not be defended, he knew, solely by the pikes and muskets of the militia; adequate strongholds in Florentine territories were likewise required. He seems to have made himself an expert in towers, bastions, and parapets, and in January he ploughed through the snow to Pisa together with the architect Giuliano da Sangallo, older brother of Antonio, whose wooden dam the militia had so staunchly defended two years earlier. The sixty-seven-year-old Giuliano had considerable experience building and repairing fortifications, both in Tuscany and latterly in Rome, where he and his brother had constructed new corner bastions on the Castel Sant' Angelo. He and Machiavelli were now to inspect the citadel at Pisa, the object of so many failed Florentine assaults, to ensure it was in a robust condition should the war between Julius II and Louis XII spill into Tuscany. From there, with a similar brief, the pair moved to Arezzo.

These surveys had assumed a special urgency since despite both the snow and the pope's illness (Julius had been suffering from a fever since the previous October) war had finally erupted between France and the Church. Rising from his sickbed in Bologna on January 2, Julius had declared, "Let's see if I've got balls as big as the king of France!" and then led his army in person through the deep snow to besiege Mirandola, a city under French protection. The Venetian envoy, witnessing the successful assault, was positively stupefied: "That a pope should come to a military camp, when he has just been ill, with so much snow and cold, in January. Historians will have something to write about!"

The Florentines were less inclined to applaud the pope's heroic exertions. The reason for their disaffection was an incident that would soon lead them into a catastrophic blunder. A month earlier, on December 22, 1510, a plot to assassinate Piero Soderini had been uncovered in Florence. The would-be assassin was a young man named Prinzivalle della Stufa. Prinzivalle's aim had been to murder the Gonfalonier in the Palazzo della Signoria and thereby clear the way for the return of the sons of Lorenzo the Magnificent to Florence. Prinzivalle managed to escape when the plot was discovered, but the Ten claimed he had named Julius as one of the architects of the plot. Julius professed innocence, but not everyone in Florence was persuaded by his denials. Soderini and his advisors soon afterward elected to follow one of Savonarola's precepts: *Gigli con gigli dover fiorire* ("Lily must with lily bloom"). That is, the French and the Florentines, both of whom took the lily as their emblem, should stick together. And so came the catastrophic blunder.

Louis XII had begun wielding ecclesiastical weapons against the pope. A number of cardinals sympathetic to the king's cause, most either Spanish or French, declared their intention to convoke a General Council—even though well-established canon law stated that only a pope could convene such a council. Cardinals, bishops, and other dignitaries and theological experts very occasionally came together in General Councils to deliberate issues of doctrine and discipline. The particular issue these cardinals wished to discuss was the removal of Julius from the Vatican and his replacement by a pope more congenial to France's presence in Italy. Precedents existed for such an action, since at the Council of Pisa, convoked in 1409, twenty-two cardinals and eighty bishops had voted to depose both Pope Gregory XII and the Spanish-born antipope Benedict XIII in favor of the Archbishop of Milan, Pietro Philarghi, who ruled as Alexander V. Alexander's successor, John XXIII, was then deposed in 1415 at one of the sessions of the Council of Constance. A similar fate—so Louis XII and his allies hoped—awaited Julius.

In January 1511, as the Warrior Pope raged through the snow to Mirandola, Louis asked the Florentine Signoria to allow the General Council to assemble in, of all places, Pisa. At first, as Julius conquered Mirandola, the Signoria equivocated. But then the plot by Prinzivalle as well as subsequent military setbacks for the pope (the French promptly recaptured Mirandola and then, in May, took Bologna) eventually prompted the Signoria to agree. In August, after Julius had returned to Rome in defeat, the Ten issued safe-conduct passes for the five cardinals who were making their way to Pisa for the council, which was due to open in September.

In allowing the council to assemble in their domains the Florentines were implicitly abandoning their customary *via di mezzo* and declaring their allegiance to Louis in preference to the pope. No sooner had they made this decision, however, than they suffered an acute failure of nerve as Julius, enraged by the temerity of the cardinals and by what he regarded as Florentine betrayal, began threatening to place the Republic under interdict. This was a powerful and damaging censure that carried more than a symbolic value: Florentine citizens would be denied all church services, the dying would not receive the sacraments, nor would the dead be allowed burial in consecrated ground. An interdict was, moreover, bad for the purse as well as the soul, since Florentine merchants would lose their legal protection everywhere in Christendom, a situation leading to the lawful plundering of their goods and monies all over Europe.

The dual threats of war and interdict prodded the Signoria into action. Machiavelli was sent urgently on his way to intercept the rebel cardinals and persuade them to turn back. He set off early in September, intercepting the cardinals, following a hard two-day ride, eighty miles north of Florence at Borgo San Donnino (present-day Fidenza). Their leader was Bernardino López de Carvajal, a fifty-six-year-old Spaniard. Machiavelli explained to him the dangers posed to Florence, but Cardinal Carvajal, who openly coveted the papal tiara, insisted that the council itself would be convoked at Pisa within two weeks, promising only not to enter Florence proper. Unable to keep the rebels from Florentine territory, Machiavelli next rode on to France. Here he was charged by the Ten with making the Florentine case before Louis XII himself. Though damaged by scandal and reviled by the *pancacce*, Machiavelli was still the man to whom the Ten and the Signoria turned in their moments of greatest crisis.

Machiavelli reached the court at Blois on September 22. The urgency of his embassy was reflected in the pace at which he rode: during the last week of his epic journey he averaged a bone-jarring sixty miles a day. He encountered little more success at Blois, though, than in Borgo San Donnino. Louis XII refused to rescind the council, although he did agree to postpone its sessions for another month, until after the Feast of All Saints. This was a small sop, but at least it provided the Florentines with a few more weeks to prepare their territories for defense—and to hope for the death of the pope or some other *deus ex machina*.

The need for some sort of mitigating development soon became desperate since, one day after Machiavelli arrived at Blois, Julius had sufficiently recovered from his illness to issue the interdict against Florence. Soon afterward he began speaking openly about killing or deposing Piero Soderini. Putting the cat squarely among the pigeons, he named Giovanni de' Medici as papal legate in Perugia. The oldest surviving son of Lorenzo the Magnificent, the thirty-five-year-old Giovanni was an influential cardinal and, since the death of Piero the Unfortunate in 1503, the standard-bearer of Medici fortunes. Julius clearly wished to throw the Florentines into turmoil and raise the hopes of the Mediceans within the city by installing on their borders the leading opponent of Soderini's government.

Machiavelli was back in Florence at the beginning of November, a few days before the Council of Pisa opened. This council soon proved itself a damp squib: though street urchins hailed Cardinal Carvajal (perhaps sarcastically) as Pope Bernardino, few Pisans, let alone any ecclesiastics, rallied to the cause of the cardinals. So hostile was their reception that Machiavelli was sent with a company of 300 of his soldiers to protect them from the populace. Within a week the Pisans' rancorous enmity succeeded where the travels and eloquence of Machiavelli had failed: Cardinal Carvajal and his cohorts began packing their trunks and preparing a move to the friendlier precincts of Milan.

The damage to Florence, however, had already been done. On his ride back from Blois in November, Machiavelli learned that Julius had signed, with Ferdinand of Aragón and the Venetians, a treaty called the Holy League. The pope hoped to use this powerful alliance to drive the French from Italy once and for all. As a Spanish army under the command of Ramón de Cardona, the Viceroy of Naples, began its march north from Rome, it became clear that Soderini's support for Louis XII and his schismatic council had succeeded only in drawing thousands of Spanish lances into Tuscany. Little wonder, then, that Machiavelli, back in Florence at the end of November, sat down and wrote his will.

If Machiavelli truly believed that no great event ever occurred in a city or province that had not been predicted by revelations, prodigies, or celestial signs, then he, like so many other people, would have been extremely concerned by reports out of Ravenna in the early months of 1512. A number of monstrous births had been reported in the city, the most horrifying of which was a creature, supposedly the offspring of a nun and a monk, that came to be known as the "monster of Ravenna." This creature looked like something out of a fresco of the Last Judgment. It had, reportedly, a horn on its head, wings like a bat, an eye on its right knee, and the birthmark of an eagle on its left foot; and it was, to cap it all, a hermaphrodite. The governor of Ravenna was so aghast that he sent a detailed description to Julius II, warning that such an unnatural issue could only betoken evil times.

The horrors foretold by the monster of Ravenna revealed themselves soon enough. On April 11, Easter Sunday, 16,000 soldiers of the Holy League commanded by Cardona met a force of 26,000 French troops two miles outside the gates of Ravenna. The French army was under the command of Gaston de Foix, a nephew of Louis XII. The twenty-three-year-old Foix was a brilliant commander known, thanks to his Borgia-like speed and unpredictability, as the "Lightning Bolt of Italy." In February he had relieved Bologna, under siege by Cardona, and then marched north to capture Brescia from the Venetians. Turning his troops around on orders from Louis XII, he began marching south toward Rome with the express purpose of invading the city and deposing the pope: his troops would soon be helping themselves, he promised them, to "the boundless riches of that wicked court" of Pope Julius. When his army paused to attack Ravenna, which housed the arsenal of the Holy League, Cardona advanced to intercept him. What followed was one of the bloodiest battles ever fought on Italian soil. More than half of Cardona's army was destroyed—as many as 9,000 men— largely by the artillery of the Duke of Ferrara, Alfonso d'Este. French losses were considerably lower but included, tragically for the French cause, Gaston de Foix himself.

The French victory at Ravenna was celebrated in Florence with the usual bonfires and illuminations and ringing of bells. As the surviving Spanish soldiers fled the carnage, it seemed the French would now march on Rome, depose Julius, and snuff out the Medici threat to Florence. Yet events stubbornly refused to hew to their seemingly inevitable course. Dispirited by the loss of Foix, the French troops made no attempt on Rome; eventually they turned around and marched north, instead of south, as 18,000 Swiss soldiers, coming to the pope's rescue, invaded French territory in Lombardy. Julius was suddenly and miraculously spared.

Florence's relations with the papacy then deteriorated further when, in June, the pope compelled the Florentine ambassador in Rome to write a letter to the Signoria relating how His Holiness desired the resignation of Piero Soderini. Should Soderini refuse, the pope would remove him by force with the armies of the Holy League. This letter was followed by an ambassador from the pope, Lorenzo Pucci, who delivered a similar threat. The matter was discussed in the Council of Eighty on July 10, but, typically, no decision was made. Four days later, a bolt of lightning struck the bell tower of the church of Santa Croce, causing great damage. "It was considered a bad omen," one Florentine murmured in his diary. As fierce thunderstorms continued to rage throughout the summer, an even worse omen followed as the Porta al Prato was struck by another bolt. Since the lightning destroyed a shield bearing a fleur-de-lis, the symbol of France, and since the Porta al Prato led to the walled town of Prato, twelve miles to the northwest, the meaning was apparent: retribution for supporting Louis XII would come to Florence by way of Prato. And at that moment, as it happened, an army of 8,000 Spaniards had begun moving south through Tuscany toward Prato. The only hope for the town—indeed, for Florence itself—appeared to be Machiavelli's militia.

Chapter Thirteen

AGOSTINO VESPUCCI ONCE observed that Machiavelli had a zeal for "riding, wandering, and roaming about." Never did Machiavelli indulge these passions so unremittingly as in the first half of 1512. He had spent the months since his return from France shuttling back and forth between Florence and the countryside, with occasional excursions to Pisa, where he mobilized a garrison for the citadel. He was conscripting not only foot soldiers but also a cavalry. He hoped to assemble several units of light horse, riders armed with lances, crossbows, and even small firearms. These men, too, were to be levied from Florentine territories, drilled by their captains, and deployed in times of need. By February of 1512 he had mustered enough of them to parade 300 horsemen in the Piazza della Signoria.

Despite the impending crisis, Machiavelli was undoubtedly relishing the exercise of his power and the uses to which his talents had been put. Seldom was he happier than when galloping into the rugged hills to review a battalion or inspect a Florentine stronghold. Such tasks, with their tangible results, were far more rewarding than serving as the agent of Florentine policies of prevarication and procrastination. The result of his energetic efforts among these farmers, stonecutters, and silkworm-breeders was, by the summer, a force of 11,000 foot soldiers and 500 horsemen.

By late summer it was clear that the mettle of Machiavelli's battalions would soon be sternly tested. Representatives of the Holy League, meeting at Mantua, decreed that the republican regime of Piero Soderini was to be destroyed and the Medici family reinstated. Ramón de Cardona's soldiers, whose overdue wages had been paid by Cardinal Giovanni's younger brother, Giuliano de' Medici, began marching south from Bologna in the middle of August. Terror spread through the countryside, and within days a mile-long procession of farmers and peasants was besieging the gates of Florence. The Madonna of Impruneta was summoned to bolster the city's morale, but the Signoria quickly rescinded the order: the times were simply too dangerous to transport that valuable relic on the open roads.

Machiavelli was sent to the quarry town of Firenzuola, twenty miles northeast of Florence, to mobilize a force of 2,000 militiamen with which to ambush the invading army as it flowed down from the Apennines. Cardona's soldiers had come through an unexpected pass, however, and neatly sidestepped the battalions to reach Barberino, only fifteen miles north of Florence. Piero Soderini, caught by surprise at the swiftness of Cardona's advance, ordered Machiavelli to make haste to Florence and prepare the city for a last stand. "Do what good you can," Biagio implored from the Chancellery.

The Spaniards, however, did not move directly on Florence. Poorly provisioned, they were unable to resupply themselves thanks to the Florentine tactic of hiding or destroying stores of fodder and foodstuffs. The only thing left to the soldiers in the deserted villages were goblets of poisoned wine. Seeking provisions for his half-starved men, Cardona moved southwest into the valley of the Bisenzio and from there, as the omen had it, toward Prato. On August 26 his herald arrived outside the gates of the city, demanding an immediate surrender and a supply of food for the soldiers. At the same time, Cardona sent ambassadors to Florence demanding further supplies. He also demanded the resignation of Soderini and the return of the exiled Medici—though strictly, he claimed, as private citizens, not as rulers.

Soderini believed he could afford defiance. He and his advisors reckoned Cardona's famished army would soon be forced to decamp. The soldiers were, moreover, as poorly provided with siege artillery as they were with bread: only two guns had been hauled south through the rugged passes. The spirits of the Florentines were further boosted by a great faith in Machiavelli's militia, which was numerically superior to Cardona's army. Eight thousand of these militiamen were garrisoned in Florence; another 3,000 had been dispatched to Prato on August 25, together with a hundred cavalry. "The men-at-arms," one Florentine wrote optimistically on August 26, "were eager to encounter the enemy . . . and had a mind to slay everyone." The militiamen arriving in Prato would have told a different story. They discovered a city that was poorly fortified and lacking both weapons and equipment. The arquebusiers were forced to strip the lead from a church roof to manufacture ammunition; even then they had no gunpowder to fire their makeshift musketballs.

As his army gathered before the walls of Prato, Cardona made a second and final offer to Florence. No longer was it necessary for Soderini to resign: all Cardona required was the return of the Medici, bread for his soldiers, and 30,000 ducats for himself—a bribe, in effect, to turn his armies around once their bellies were full and the Medici back in their palace. The Florentines had been happy enough in the past to use ducats to safeguard their liberty. Soderini was urged by his advisors—Machiavelli probably among them—to assent to Cardona's terms. However, the Gonfalonier was still relying on the hunger pangs of the Spaniards, the strength of the militia, and (according to Machiavelli) "certain vain opinions." Cardona, losing patience, began bombarding the walls of Prato with his two feeble cannons. One of the weapons soon burst, but a day later the second opened a gap in the wall. At six o'clock in the evening the Spaniards mounted their scaling ladders and poured through the breach. It was August 29: the feast of, appropriately, the Decollation (i.e., the beheading) of John the Baptist, the patron saint of Florence. What followed was, in Francesco Guicciardini's account, "no longer any resistance, but only cries, flight, violence, sack, blood and killings."

The brutal sack of Prato was a calamity of the greatest

magnitude for Machiavelli. His 3,000 militiamen disgraced themselves by throwing down their weapons and fleeing. The Spaniards were amazed, according to Guicciardini, that military men "should show such cowardice and so little skill." Or, as another appalled Florentine put it, they "all became as timid as mice." As many as 4,000 people were killed inside the walls of Prato, roughly half of them members of the militia, the rest defenseless Pratesi. Others suffered terrible atrocities at the hands of Cardona's men. Lamenting the "pitiable spectacle of calamity" in Prato, Machiavelli himself alluded to the horrific nature of these crimes: "Nor did they spare the virgins cloistered in holy sites, which were all filled with acts of rape and pillage."

Machiavelli's great dream had failed spectacularly. The citizen militia in which he had invested more than six years of hope and toil had proved itself an even bigger disaster than the futile canal or the unreliable and unscrupulous *condottieri*. His faith in the courage and trustworthiness of a citizen army had proved itself the flimsiest of illusions. The people of Prato had paid for this delusion in blood. Florence, it now appeared, would pay the price with its liberty.

News of the sack of Prato, when it reached Florence, caused "great perturbation in the minds of men." No one was more perturbed than Piero Soderini. According to Guicciardini, the Gonfalonier was "terrified . . . having almost completely lost his reputation and prestige." The crisis made him irresolute and slack-spined, and when, on August 31, a group of Medici supporters stormed the Palazzo della Signoria and demanded his resignation, he broke into tears and threatened suicide. Machiavelli was the man to whom he then turned in his hour of need. The Second Chancellor, summoned to the Palazzo della Signoria, arranged for his friend to be transported safely into exile. A day later, Giuliano de' Medici rode trimphantly into Florence.

The thirty-three-year-old Giuliano had spent most of his exile at the court in Urbino. He was, like his father, Lorenzo, an elegant courtier rather than a warrior. A portrait of him painted by Raphael a few years later would show a slim young man with a long neck, a sparse beard, and a flamboyant hat tipped at a jaunty angle. He would likewise be immortalized by Baldassare Castiglione in *The Book of the Courtier*, which celebrated him for his "goodness, nobility and courtesy." Though only fifteen when the Medici were expelled from Florence, by then he had already made the acquaintance of Machiavelli, who seems to have composed a poem in his honor and belonged, however briefly or peripherally, to the circle of his father. Machiavelli therefore had some reason to expect that, despite his reputation as Soderini's right-hand man, he would not suffer unduly from the return of the Medici.

At first it seemed as though the city would remain peaceful, with few changes in its government. On September 3, Florence joined the Holy League, agreeing to the return of the Medici as private citizens and paying 40,000 ducats to Cardona. A few days later, the Signoria elected a new Gonfalonier, Giovanbattista Ridolfi, a leading member of the *ottimati* and a longtime opponent of Soderini; his term of office was intended to last fourteen months. At this point it looked as if the Medici had been successfully assimilated into the Republic, which would be governed much as before. "The city is quiet and peaceful," Machiavelli wrote soon after Soderini's flight, "and hopes, with the help of these Medici, to live no less honoured than it did in times past, when their father, Lorenzo the Magnificent, of most happy memory, governed."

This situation was not to last, thanks to, as Guicciardini complained, "disagreements among the citizens" as well as the tempting presence, for Medici partisans, of the Spanish soldiers. In the middle of September a group of young Medici supporters—Soderini's would-be assassin, Prinzivalle della Stufa, among them—engineered a swift *coup d'état*. Dismayed by the election of Ridolfi, whom they regarded as too moderate, they and Giuliano de' Medici entered the Palazzo della Signoria with weapons concealed beneath their cloaks. At a given signal, the great bell in the tower known as *La Vacca* was rung, an alarm that for two centuries had summoned Florentine men into the piazza. The piazza also flooded, however, with Spanish soldiers. A decree was read to the populace from the *ringhiera*, beside Michelangelo's *David*, and the Florentines found themselves obliged to accept, at the tips of Spanish steel, the dissolution of the Great Council and the establishment of a ruling council of forty citizens—all Medici loyalists—who would be given absolute authority. Florence was now a republic in name only: the real power would reside not in the Palazzo della Signoria but a short distance away at the Palazzo Medici.

The new lords of Florence were Giuliano and his older brother, Cardinal Giovanni.

Machiavelli's legacy was swiftly and utterly dismantled. His militia was disarmed and disbanded, and the Nine Officials of the Florentine Ordnance and Militia dissolved. Yet for the time being he remained in his post as Second Chancellor. Little is known of his activities then, but sometime in October he took the time to offer unbidden advice to the Mediceans. He wrote the *Ricordo ai palleschi*, or "Memorandum to the Medici Supporters," a kind of open letter in which he argued that denigrating Piero Soderini's regime in order to flatter the new Medici lords would be a counterproductive exercise that might lead to—and this was wishful thinking in the extreme—a restoration of Soderini's government. He also wrote a letter to Cardinal Giovanni (also known to him, no doubt, from Lorenzo's circle) in response to the appointment at the end of September of five officials to inventory the property confiscated from the Medici in 1494. Machiavelli warned the cardinal that the reappropriation of these properties and possessions would come at the cost of alienating much of the populace. Cardinal Giovanni paid little heed: the confiscated property was returned to Medici hands.

Whatever their past relations, by 1512 neither Giuliano nor Cardinal Giovanni would have been especially well-disposed toward the Second Chancellor. Machiavelli had taken a hard line against the family in 1508, when a marriage was arranged between Filippo Strozzi (a member of a distinguished Florentine family) and Clarice de' Medici, the fifteen-year-old daughter of the late Piero the Unfortunate. The proposed marriage was seen by Soderini, who opposed the match, as a plot by which the Medici would gain support from the powerful Strozzi for their return to Florence. The match was denounced by Machiavelli, who took a particularly intransigent line, arguing that since Piero was a rebel against Florence, all his line were to be considered rebels, his young daughter included. The Eight of the Watch, deciding the case, found in favor of Clarice, and the marriage took place in 1509. Giuliano and Cardinal Giovanni would hardly, though, have forgotten Machiavelli's vehement opposition to their family and his eloquent denunciation of their niece. Words spoken by Piero Soderini must have been ringing in Machiavelli's ears in the days since Giuliano de' Medici appeared in Florence. In a speech to the Great Council at the end of August, Soderini had warned that if the Medici returned to Florence their rule would be a severe and vindictive one marked by suspicion and retribution: they would not forget, he predicted, "their exile and the harsh manner in which they had been treated."

Machiavelli had seen the purge of Savonarola's supporters from office in 1498, and he was present in Rome in 1503 as Julius II ruthlessly settled scores with Cesare Borgia. He cannot therefore have been taken too much aback when, on November 7, he was deprived of his post in the Chancellery. A Signoria dominated by Mediceans decreed that he should be "dismissed, deprived and totally removed." His position was immediately assumed by Niccolò Michelozzi, a Medici loyalist and former secretary to Lorenzo the Magnificent. Three days later, on November 10, Machiavelli was confined to Florentine territories and forced to post a bond of a thousand gold ducats, a huge sum (the equivalent of almost eight years of his salary) that obliged him to turn to friends for a loan. But the Medici and their supporters were not yet finished with him: a week later he was banned for a year from setting foot inside the Palazzo della Signoria.

Machiavelli's political career had come to an abrupt end. Leaving his office in the Chancellery for the last time, he may well have paused to reflect on the fresco of the Wheel of Fortune above the doorway of the Hall of the Lilies. The capricious goddess had indeed turned against him.

Chapter Fourteen

MACHIAVELLI WAS FORTY-THREE years old in 1512. If he, like the Medici, took inventory of everything that had been confiscated from him, he must have felt he had little to show for his many years of service to the Republic. He was banned from the building that for almost fifteen years had been his home much more than the Casa Machiavelli across the river. Worse still, the man who was so addicted to "riding, wandering, and roaming about" was confined to Florentine dominions, with no outlet for his energies, skills, and ambitions. Perhaps worst of all, he, like Soderini, had lost his reputation and prestige.

Machiavelli's sacking must have been made more grievous by the knowledge that he and Biagio Buonaccorsi were the only members of the Chancellery to lose their posts. The fact that Machiavelli's dismissal was not part of a clean sweep in the Palazzo della Signoria indicated the level of his unpopularity—and not just with the Mediceans and the *ottimati*. Over the years he had alienated many Florentine businessmen and politicians, first with his arrogance and abrasiveness, and then with scandalous behavior that became the fodder for so much gossip. Finally, the drastic dereliction of his vaunted militia in Florence's hour of direst need seemed to prove the worthlessness of both this pet project and, more generally, his abilities as a leader. The plaudits won on the Fiume Morto in 1509 had turned, three years later, into widespread grumbling about folly and incompetence.[1] Still, if he felt that autumn that his situation could not get any worse, he was sadly mistaken: within months he was arrested and thrown into prison.

Machiavelli's arrest came on the night of February 18, 1513. He was one of about a dozen men arrested by the Eight of the Watch in connection with an assassination plot against Giuliano de' Medici. The plot was discovered when a piece of paper listing some twenty conspirators was accidentally dropped by the supposed ringleader, Agostino Capponi, a young man from one of Florence's most prominent families. The seventh name on Capponi's list was Machiavelli's. Arrested along with Capponi and other supposed conspirators, he was taken to the Stinche, an ancient prison near the church of Santa Croce. Ominously, this was the very prison in which his distant relative, Francesco Machiavelli, his father's second cousin, had been beheaded in 1459 for his opposition to Cosimo de' Medici. It now looked possible that the Medici ax would terminate the political career of another Machiavelli.[2]

Machiavelli was certainly not averse to political assassination, especially if it meant the deliverance of a city or state from tyranny. But his involvement in the plot by Agostino Capponi was peripheral to say the least. He did know a number of the conspirators, one of whom was Niccolò Valori, a former ambassador to France who was a long-standing friend. Yet if he shared their confidence, he seems not to have participated actively in their conspiracy. Under interrogation by the Eight, one of the conspirators, another intimate named Giovanni Folchi, confessed to having approached Machiavelli regarding the plot. Given his rough treatment at their hands, Machiavelli could reasonably have been expected to support a conspiracy against the Medici: the removal of Giuliano de' Medici and the toppling of his regime would open the way for his return to government.

Yet Machiavelli does not seem to have offered the conspirators any assistance or support. According to Folchi's confession, he simply replied that the present government might soon founder of its own accord because—and here he took a swipe at Giuliano de' Medici—the lack of a figure such as Lorenzo the Magnificent meant there was no one "to stand at the tiller."[3] The comment hardly attests to a belief that Florence's salvation lay at the point of a dagger. Even so, the disparaging comments about Giuliano did nothing to help his case, and he was apparently taken to the torture chamber and subjected to a device called the *strappado* (from *strappare*, to rip or tear). This technique involved binding the victim's arms behind his back with a pulleyed rope and then dropping him from a height such that, as the rope jerked tight, his shoulders were dislocated. Machiavelli apparently survived six of these drops without incriminating himself. He later wrote that his intestinal fortitude made him "consider myself more of a man than I believed I was."

Five days after his arrest, as he lay shackled in his cell, Machiavelli was awakened by noises outside the prison. To the north of the Stinche lay the Via de' Malcontenti, thus named for being the road along which condemned criminals were led for execution. The condemned were always accompanied on their doleful journeys by black-hooded members of the Confraternità dei Neri, the "Black Brothers," who devoted themselves to consoling the condemned by chanting funeral hymns and holding before their eyes painted images of the Crucifixion. On the morning of February 23 the Black Brothers were singing psalms for two of the conspirators, Capponi and a young albino named Pietropaolo Boscoli. Carried in carts along the Via de' Malcontenti, the pair were beheaded at ten o'clock in the morning in the Pratello della Giustizia (Field of Justice).

Machiavelli, in fear for his own life, showed no sympathy for Capponi and Boscoli: "Now let them go, I pray," he wrote to Giuliano de' Medici, "if only your mercy may turn towards me." These words were part of a twenty-line poem, a kind of "prison sonnet" composed as an appeal for clemency while he awaited his own fate. Describing himself as a poet (an attempt, presumably, to kindle memories of his days at Lorenzo the Magnificent's court), he laments discomforts such as the six drops of the *strappado* and the discomfort of his shackles. "My other misfortunes I shall not tell," he says, before proceeding to enumerate them at length: the stench of his cell, the size of its lice, the sounds of prisoners being tortured in neighboring cells. The poem ends with Machiavelli hearing the Black Brothers and then making his pitiless remarks about Capponi and Boscoli.[4]

The cynical and coldhearted lines at the end of the poem have caused some of Machiavelli's biographers to recoil in horror and embarrassment, or else to excuse their subject by suggesting that he wrote the words (as one of them claimed) "in a moment of bad humor." This same biographer, Pasquale Villari, even ventured that Machiavelli was led to such a wicked sentiment "by the dictates of rhyme." The poem is less revealing of Machiavelli's views about the treatment of Capponi and Boscoli, though, than it is about his own treatment in the Stinche. It is odd that so many of Machiavelli's biographers should have regarded this poetic exercise as an accurate record of historical fact. In fact, the work is full of literary conceits (as one would expect in a poem) that cast into serious doubt any literal reading of Machiavelli's experience. Trained in the art of eloquence, he uses a whole range of rhetorical strategies—techniques outlined in works such as Cicero's *De inventione*—to frame his language and his argument in ways that will evoke feelings of pity and mercy.

The work opens with the exordium—the plea to Giuliano, addressed by name—and ends with the peroratio, the final appeal by which the speaker or writer makes his graceful retreat: "Surpass the name of your father and your grandfather." Along the way Machiavelli employs several rhetorical figures. According to the poem, the lice in the cell are as big as butterflies and the smell worse than Roncesvalles—a reference to the battlefield in the French epic poem, *The Song of Roland*. The sound of the padlocks, keys, and bolts are, claims the poet, like Jove hurling thunderbolts to earth from the top of "Mongibello," a local name for Mount Etna. These are more than ordinary hyperbole; they are ornate literary allusions. He also uses ironic understatement, calling his cell a *delicato ostello*, or a "dainty hospice." His pretended omission ("my other misfortunes I shall not tell") is a textbook example of paralipsis, a trope known to him from (among other places) *Rhetoric to Herennius*. This classic work, thought during the Renaissance to have been written by Cicero, offered the prototypical example of a speaker or writer pretending to gloss over—while in fact emphasizing—something unpleasant: "I pass by your thefts and robberies."

Written in the vernacular, the poem is full of sophisticated literary as well as rhetorical devices. Machiavelli makes use, for example, of alliteration: in the space of a few lines he piles up *poeti* (poets), *parieti* (walls), *pidocchi* (lice), *paffuti* (well-fed) and *puzzo* (stench). He also uses enclosed rhymes, that is, the same rhyme scheme employed by Petrarch in his sonnets, with the octet running ABBA ABBA. Most of the poem is, like Petrarch's sonnets, in iambic pentameter, and it includes a number of clever rhymes: *farfalle* (butterflies) with Roncesvalles. All of which amply justify Machiavelli's description of himself, in the fourth line, as a poet.

The poem is thus neither a literal description of his prison conditions nor a few lines of doggerel scribbled in a moment of bad humor. It is a technically accomplished piece of verse whose rhetorical ploys and literary allusions raise the question of how such a work could have been composed by someone shackled and tortured in a filthy cell. Torture was of course widely used in Florence. Techniques included not just the *strappado* but also the rack and a method in which the soles of the feet were flayed and then burned with hot coals. There is no doubt that both Capponi and Boscoli would have been subjected to various of these brutal measures. But is Machiavelli's account in his poem of six drops of the *strappado* merely one more piece of hyperbole, such as his description of the size of the lice and the sound of the padlocks? The first few drops of the rope suffered by Savonarola (he was given a total of fourteen over the course of a month in 1498) left his muscles torn and his mind so deranged that no meaningful confessions could be extracted by his torturers. One of the other friars imprisoned with Savonarola, Fra Domenico, described the terrible effects of the *strappado* on himself: "I am all shattered, and my arms are useless, especially the left, which by this [torture] is now dislocated for the second time."[5] Still, whatever the nature or extent of his torture, there is no doubt Machiavelli showed as much courage as literary skill during his confinement. It is unclear, though, whether his well-wrought poem—this eloquent plea for mercy—ever reached Giuliano de' Medici or, if so, whether it had any effect on him.

Early in the morning of March 11, 1513, Machiavelli would have been awakened in his cell by the sound of tolling bells and a loud cannonade. Pope Julius II had died on February 21, a few days after Machiavelli's arrest, and in the conclave that followed, Cardinal Giovanni de' Medici, at the age of only thirty-seven, was elected Pope Leo X. The five days of celebration that followed far exceeded anything ever seen in Florence. Cannons were fired in continuous salute, the Palazzo della Signoria was illuminated with burning wine barrels, and triumphal carriages were paraded through the streets to the front of the Palazzo Medici. So great was the city's joy that even the women—usually shut safely away—appeared at the windows of houses. People soon began throwing their signboards, floorboards, and furniture into the flames in this frenzy of celebration; some even stripped the timbers from the roofs of their shops. "It seemed as though the city was upside-down," wrote an amazed Florentine.

Machiavelli was saved from further torture and imprisonment—and possibly even execution—by this *deus ex machina*. He was released from prison, as part of a general amnesty, on March 11 or 12, following some three weeks of imprisonment. As he crossed over the Ponte Vecchio to the Casa Machiavelli amid the tumult of cannons and bells, the clouds of smoke, and the crackle of burning timbers, he might have believed, like everyone else, that a Golden Age was dawning for Florence. A Florentine, the son of Lorenzo the Magnificent, was in the Vatican. It was by no means clear, though, what this new world might hold for the ex-prisoner Niccolò Machiavelli.

How did Machiavelli celebrate his liberation from the Stinche? In a letter to a friend in Rome, dated March 18, he wrote how he was "marking time during these general festivities, enjoying the remainder of this life." The enjoyment of life meant one thing in particular to Machiavelli: "Every day we visit the house of some girl to recover our vigor," he wrote lightheartedly. He even boasted to his friend about how he had watched the barefoot procession of the Madonna of Impruneta—brought to Florence in thanks for the election of Leo X—from the window of a prostitute named Sandra di Pero.

This friend in Rome was Francesco Vettori, with whom Machiavelli had served at the court of Maximilian in the first few months of 1508. Vettori would have seemed, at first glance, a natural enemy for Machiavelli. His family were staunch Mediceans (his father had been an ambassador under Lorenzo the Magnificent) and they were related by both blood and marriage to some of the grandest of the *ottimati*. Machiavelli had, nonetheless, found Vettori an appealing companion, someone who enjoyed a good joke as well as (to judge from the numerous enthusiastic references in his correspondence) the society of prostitutes.

Vettori had risen in the world since his days with Machiavelli in Innsbruck, not least because his brother, Paolo, was a close friend of Giuliano de' Medici. At the end of December 1512 Vettori had been appointed Florentine ambassador to the Vatican, a position he formally assumed early in February. By this time the pair had become such close companions that Vettori left Florence on a horse borrowed from Machiavelli. Emerging from the dungeon in search of a position, Machiavelli therefore turned, naturally enough, to his friend. He wrote to Rome urging Vettori to find his brother Totto (who had been ordained as a priest in 1509, and who was likewise bombarding Vettori with pleas for assistance) a position on Pope Leo's staff. He was then bold enough to inquire about his own prospects with the Medici: "If it is possible, remind Our Lordship about me in order that, if it should be possible, either he or his family might start engaging my services in some way or other, because I believe I shall do honor to you and do something useful for me." It is a poignant and rather desperate plea from someone who had so recently been a man of such consequence.

Vettori vowed to do anything within his powers to increase his friend's "honor and profit." But the situation was a delicate one, and in April he confessed he could find positions for neither Machiavelli nor his brother. The only promise he could make was that, if Machiavelli joined him in Rome, "we shall not fail to get a girl whom I have near my house and spend some time with her." Not even this offer could cheer Machiavelli, whose spirits had begun to slump. In the middle of April he wrote back to Vettori, still desperate to gain employment and incredulous that the Medici would ignore a man of his talents: "I cannot believe that if only His Holiness began to put me to work, I would not help myself and bring utility and honour to all my friends." But Vettori was either unwilling or, more likely, unable to assist. Innocent he may have been in the Capponi-Boscoli conspiracy, but Machiavelli was persona non grata nonetheless at the court of the Medici.

Even so, at this time Machiavelli exerted himself to try to win favor with the Medici. With his quill still sharp from his sonnet to Giuliano de' Medici, he wrote the words to "Song of the Blessed Spirits." Carnivals and carnival songs had once been an important part of Florentine cultural life. The reign of Lorenzo the Magnificent had witnessed the celebration of the Calendimaggio, a riotous May Day festival that featured pageants, floats, and parades in which performers in costumes and masks danced in the streets and sang madrigals. Some of these songs were composed by Machiavelli's friend Heinrich Isaac; others were penned by the greatest poet of the age, Angelo Poliziano, and still others by Lorenzo himself. The Calendimaggio had disappeared with the death of Lorenzo and the rise of Savonarola, though it returned, in a somewhat muted form, after 1498. The reappearance of the Medici in Florence promised a revival of festivals in general, and of the Calendimaggio in particular.

In "Song of the Blessed Spirits," Machiavelli devoted his poetical talents to celebrating the ascension of Leo X and, so the song dared to hope, a long period of peace. It is unclear whether the song was ever actually performed in public; if so, those accustomed to the drolleries of "Machia"—and of the playful levity of carnival songs in general, which usually celebrated such things as the coming of May and the unsurpassed beauty of Florentine women—would have been surprised by the earnestness and even despondency of the almost dirgelike verse that laments

The pitiable and cruel affliction of miserable mortals
Their long distress and suffering without remedy

Their lament for countless ills that for day and night
Make them complain with sobs and distress
With loud voices and sorrowful outcry.[6]

These doleful sentiments indicate just how out of step the increasingly disillusioned Machiavelli was with the jubilant spirit of the times. His gloom as the spring of 1513 blossomed may likewise be glimpsed in the lines from one of Petrarch's sonnets that he chose to include in a letter to Vettori:

Therefore, if at times I laugh or sing
I do so because I have no other way than this
To give vent to my bitter tears.

This letter was dated April 16, two weeks before the Calendimaggio. If Machiavelli wrote "Song of the Blessed Spirits" for the 1513 festival, he did not stay in Florence to hear it performed. At the end of April he left the city for his farm at Sant' Andrea in Percussina. By this time it was obvious that none of his efforts to recommend himself to the Medici had borne the slightest fruit. And so here in the hills south of Florence, with no other prospects in sight, he would suffer his cruel martyrdom and weep his bitter tears.

Chapter Fifteen

THE VILLAGE OF Sant' Andrea in Percussina was on the ancient Via Romana, seven miles south of Florence and two miles north of the fortified hilltop town of San Casciano. In 1513 it featured a small church, a tavern, a well, a butcher shop, a mill, a tower with small houses clustered about, and a larger stone house—the Machiavelli residence—whose dubious amenities had earned it the name the Albergaccio, or the "wretched inn." Across the road from the Albergaccio stood a small house for the farmhand and his family, as well as an olive-press, a bakehouse, a shed for livestock, and a house that had been adapted for wine production. Beyond this small array of buildings, running down a slope of hill to a river, stretched the remainder of what Machiavelli called his "minuscule patrimony": olive groves, pastureland, a vineyard, and an oak wood called "Caffagio." Far in the distance, but still clearly visible from the garden of the Albergaccio, was the dome of Santa

Maria del Fiore and—such was the terrible spite of Fortune—the belltower of the Palazzo della Signoria.

Machiavelli installed himself in this beautiful but rustic environment, depressed and disillusioned, at the end of April. Here he dwelt, as he wrote to Francesco Vettori, "removed from any human face." That was not quite true. With him was Marietta, his wife of twelve years, now heavily pregnant with their seventh child. One of their children had died in infancy in 1506, but there remained three sons (Bernardo, Lodovico, and Guido) and two daughters (Primerana and Bartolomea). "Marietta and all of us are well," he wrote in June to his nephew Giovanni, the son of his late sister Primavera. A month later Marietta gave birth to a daughter, who died soon afterward. The death weighed heavily on Machiavelli's already oppressed spirits. "Physically I feel well," he wrote to Giovanni at the beginning of August, announcing the little girl's death, "but ill in every other respect. No other hope remains for me but that God may help me." It was at this point, in the summer of 1513, that, sitting at his desk in the Albergaccio, he took up his quill and began composing a work quite different from his verses to the Medici. Machiavelli was about to make a virtue of necessity.

According to Petrarch, an enforced retirement in a rural setting was not without its benefits. The praises of a house in the country had already been sung by ancient Roman writers such as Pliny the Younger. Petrarch enthusiastically took up the theme in *De vita solitaria* (On the Solitary Life), arguing that scholarship and contemplation required a withdrawal from the haunts of men to a serene life of Arcadian repose. Machiavelli preferred cities and the active life more than almost any man on earth; yet, as he explained in a letter to Vettori on December 10, he had begun making the most of his sedate life in Sant' Andrea in Percussina. Though his existence was one of boredom, troubles, and the fear of poverty and death, he had been rescued from his cares by studying and writing about what he had earlier called "the action of men and their ways of doing things."

The prompt for Machiavelli's letter had been one he received from Vettori a short while earlier. "I have decided to describe to you what my life in Rome is like," Vettori began. What followed was a chronicle of the typical day in the life of an ambassador in Rome. Vettori's days were spent, apparently, in a whirl of lavish entertainments ("three or four courses, eating out of silver dishes"), audiences with the pope, conversations with cardinals, and visits from distinguished out-of-town guests to his commodious house near the Vatican. His only regret was that, since moving house, "I am no longer near as many courtesans as I was last summer."

This ebullient account smacks of someone gorging himself in front of a starving man, but Machiavelli took no offense. "I want to repay you in the same coin," he wrote back amiably in his letter of December 10. He then proceeded to offer a detailed recital of how his own days and nights were passed in his unwilling exile from the haunts of men.[1]

Machiavelli's typical day, as he describes it, begins before dawn. His first task is to put food on the table, so he mixes birdlime—a sticky substance usually made from fermented holly bark—and heads into his woods with a bundle of bird-cages on his back. Smearing these traps with his adhesive, he will come away with "at least two, at most six, thrushes." Other diversions follow: chopping firewood and gossiping with his woodsmen, then going to a leafy bower with a volume of Dante or Petrarch "or one of the minor poets" under his arm to read about their "amorous passions" while pleasingly recollecting his own. Next, making his way back to Sant' Andrea in Percussina, he calls in at the tavern beside the Albergaccio for chit-chat with travelers who have stopped to refresh themselves. By then the time has come for the noon meal, the *comesto*, which he eats with his family in the Albergaccio. (A model of self-sufficiency, he furnishes his table with nothing but the yield from his gardens, fields, and pastures.) After lunch he returns to the tavern to while away the afternoon hours with a band of locals: the innkeeper, a butcher, a miller, and several workers from a nearby brick kiln. They play a card game called *cricca* (illegal in Florence until fifty years earlier) and *tric-trac*, a board game similar to backgammon. These games are eagerly contested, leading to "thousands of squabbles and endless abuses and vituperations." The tragic plight of a former Second Chancellor of the Republic of Florence throwing dice and moving his checkers across a backgammon board in a rural tavern is not lost on Machiavelli, who stops to wonder whether "fate is ashamed of treating me so."

Machiavelli returns home from these tumultuous games of chance at nightfall. Only now does his day truly begin. His letter offers Vettori a glimpse of the real solace he has found in his contemplative life. The boredom and idle distraction give way as, entering his study, he removes his grubby workday clothes and dresses himself, as in the old days, in "the garments of court and palace." Thus attired, he enters "the venerable courts of the ancients"—the worlds of men such as Alexander the Great, Xenophon, and Julius Caesar—and nourishes himself "on that food that *alone* is mine and for which I was born." He converses with these age-old rulers, questioning them about the motives behind their actions, while they, "out of their human kindness, answer me. And for four hours at a time I feel no boredom, I forget all my troubles, I do not dread poverty, and I am not terrified by death. I absorb myself into them completely." But that is not all, Machiavelli tells Vettori. Taking up his pen, he has "jotted down what I have profited from in their conversation," and these perceptions he has turned into a "short study" called *De principatibus* (On Principalities).

This was Machiavelli's first known reference to the work that was to become *The Prince*. He probably began the study in August, while marooned in the deepest doldrums, and it was virtually completed, thanks to his enforced leisure, by the time he wrote his letter to Vettori in the second week of December. He hoped to send the manuscript to Vettori, partly for his opinion but mostly because he wanted his friend to present it to Giuliano de' Medici, to whom he planned to dedicate it. Giuliano, he believed, would benefit from its wisdom: "Through this study of mine, were it to be read, it would be evident that during the fifteen years I have been studying the art of the state I have neither slept nor fooled around, and anybody ought to be happy to utilize someone"—he finished optimistically—"who has so much experience."

Vettori wrote back on Christmas Eve politely asking to see the manuscript. Machiavelli immediately sent a substantial chunk to Rome: the remainder he was still "fattening and currying." Vettori's response to what he read was, at best, lukewarm. In a letter of January 18 he admitted to having enjoyed what he read but, not having seen the entire work, decided to withhold his judgment about whether or not it should be presented to Giuliano. Vettori, typically, was much more interested in discussing his experiences with a young woman named Costanza, the twenty-year-old daughter of his neighbor. "I have become almost a prisoner of this Costanza," he swooned. "I shall be so bold as to say that you never set eyes on a more beautiful woman, nor a more seductive one." Hiding his disappointment at his friend's reply, Machiavelli wrote back with some advice on how to manage Costanza. It was advice that he himself was striving hard to follow; and it was advice that—if the world would only listen—he was hoping to offer to princes, since his precepts for statecraft differed little from his prescription for success in love: "Face Fortune squarely," he wrote to Vettori, "and follow whatever course both the revolving heavens and the conditions sent you by the times and by mankind lay at your doorstep."

Fortune and the revolving heavens soon laid more tribulations at Machiavelli's doorstep. Several months later, in May, he pressed an evasive Vettori for his honest opinion: should the work be sent to Giuliano or not? Vettori, having perhaps made inquiries in Rome, reluctantly answered in the negative. Once more Machiavelli's hopes had been cruelly thwarted. In a letter to Vettori dated June 10 he angrily described his situation as one in which he was "rotting away . . . unable to find any man who recalls my service or believes I might be good for anything." His work on princes and principalities may have beguiled him for a few hours each evening, helping him to overcome feelings of worthlessness and depression; but it appeared as though it would serve no further purpose. The short study was set aside to gather dust.

Why did Francesco Vettori decline to present the work to Giuliano de' Medici? Was Machiavelli too inescapably an outcast at the Medici court? Or did Vettori realize the potential for controversy in so original and revolutionary a work?

Vettori would have recognized immediately that *The Prince* was part of an extensive literary tradition, that of "mirrors for princes." *On Kingship* by Thomas Aquinas and *The Government of Princes* by Giles of Rome, both from the thirteenth century, were two of the more famous examples. These were handbooks that offered political guidance to budding heads of state. Like them, *The Prince* takes as its subject what Machiavelli called "the art of the state." It gives instructions on how to govern princedoms, with special reference to those territories acquired through "the arms and fortunes of others."[2] Machiavelli's particular interest in how to consolidate power won in this fashion—as opposed to how to rule a hereditary principality—was no doubt inspired by the fact that the Medici had returned to

Florence thanks to good fortune and Spanish lances. The work should therefore have carried a singular pertinence for Giuliano de' Medici. Even so, the work bears much more than just a local Florentine interest. In the course of 30,000 words, Machiavelli ranges widely and knowledgeably over several thousand years of history, scrutinizing the actions of rulers such as Hannibal, Alexander the Great, and Agathocles, the brutal tyrant of Syracuse. He also includes many recent events from Italian history, with Cesare Borgia taking a starring role.

The treatise offers a good deal of practical advice. Machiavelli suggests how a citizen militia (whose advantage over mercenary armies is made clear) should be organized; whether or not fortresses are useful; why the system of taxation must not be changed; and how a prince should go about choosing his ministers and treating his minions. He does not shy away from tendering counsel of the most hard-boiled variety: if a new prince wishes to keep hold of his possessions, he warns, then the deposed ruler and his entire family must be slain. The work concludes with a passionate appeal for the "illustrious" House of Medici to become the savior of Italy—to rescue her from "those barbarous cruelties and outrages" perpetrated by foreign occupiers.

However numerous the precedents for a treatise on princely government, Machiavelli had produced something entirely new: though his subject "has often been written about before," he notes, previous authors have always discussed matters too abstractedly and impracticably. He is not interested in how his arguments will work on the page but how they might serve at court, in the piazza, or on the battlefield. He claims to "represent things as they are in a real truth, rather than as they are imagined." The result of his inquiries is "an original set of rules." And it is the nature of some of these rules that may well have alarmed Vettori.

At the heart of *The Prince* are the philosophical questions with which Machiavelli had wrestled in his letters to Bartolomeo Vespucci in 1503 and Giovan Battista Soderini three years later. These earlier letters had been his bewildered response to the inexplicable fortunes and misfortunes of Cesare Borgia and Julius II. But by the time he was unhappily ensconced at Sant' Andrea in Percussina in 1513, the question of how to counteract "bad fortune"—how to rise in the world when Fortune was against you—had an unavoidably personal dimension. Machiavelli was trying to discover for himself as much as for the book's intended recipient, Giuliano de' Medici, how to face Fortune squarely and follow the course vouchsafed by the revolving heavens.

When Machiavelli writes about Fortune, he is not speaking metaphorically. Medieval Christians such as Dante had understood Fortune as a divine (and specifically feminine) force created by God at the same time as the angels who govern the heavens. In Canto VII of the *Inferno*, for example, he describes Fortune as a "general minister and guide" who doles out good and bad luck more or less unpredictably and inexplicably. Boccaccio in the *Decameron* likewise devotes much thought to the erratic and pitiless nature of Fortune, and one of his narrators speaks for the majority of medieval philosophers when she claims that Fortune "arranges and rearranges" human affairs in "her own inscrutable fashion . . . without following any discernible plan."[3] This lack of a discernible plan meant, for upholders of this view, that men were both powerless to counteract Fortune and foolish to trust in her. The lesson for medieval Christians was a plain one: trust not in the things of this world, but lay up your store in heaven instead.

A different view of Fortune also existed, however. In 1353 Petrarch had composed a treatise titled *De remediis utriusque fortunae* (Remedies Against Good and Bad Luck) in which he argued that men were not in fact helpless before Fortune, and that they could arm themselves against her (though he was careful to warn his readers not to entrust their happiness to worldly success). This more optimistic view of man's abilities was developed by a number of later writers, including the Neapolitan poet and scholar Giovanni Pontano. In about the year 1500 Pontano wrote *On Fortune*, arguing that, although Fortune was unpredictable and even malicious, her power could be overcome through courageous, flexible, and prudent action. Pontano stressed that prudence, and not Fortune, was the true "helmsman" in human life. So widespread had this view become among humanists that by 1510 Sir Thomas More could write a poem, "The Book of Fortune," in which Lady Fortune complains of the "deadly foes" who have written "many a book / To my dispraise."

This "dispraise" of Fortune announces man's new place in the cosmic order. No longer the hapless plaything of powerful and unpredictable forces, he has become an agent of action capable of resisting and even turning the tide of events. This belief that man was free to shape his own destiny—that he possessed the power, as Pico wrote, "to have what he chooses, to be what he wills to be"—came largely from the writers of classical antiquity. The Romans' faith in men's abilities to sway Fortune was exemplified by the fact that, as Plutarch noted, they built more temples to Fortune than to any of their other gods. They believed that Fortune could best be wooed—like a flesh-and-blood woman—by a man showing certain desirable qualities such as courage and resourcefulness. Virgil in Book X of the *Aeneid* puts into the mouth of the Italian hero Turnus a rousing prebattle speech that ends: "Fortune favors the brave." By Virgil's time, the first century B.C., this slogan had become something of a truism in Latin literature. The steadfast behavior that could turn the head or melt the heart of Fortune was embodied in the Roman concept of *virtus* (from the Latin *vir*, the "man of true manliness"), a cultural value encompassing toughness, bravery, and a never-say-die willingness to combat adversity. The concept was translated into Italian as *virtù*, with Petrarch claiming in *De remediis utriusque fortunae*—one of his most popular and widely read books—that *virtù* was the best antidote against the caprices of Fortune. The Italian word did not imply the moral worthiness of the English word "virtue" so much as the masculine prowess of its other cognate, "virility."

Taking up the humanist concept of *virtù* in *The Prince*, Machiavelli decides that Fortune's spinning wheel can—to some extent at least—be steered or controlled. The gloomy determinism of his 1506 letter to Giovan Battista Soderini gives way in *The Prince* to a slightly more upbeat view of human action. In order "not to rule out our free will," he arrives at a formula by which Fortune is "the arbiter of half the things we do, leaving the other half or so to be controlled by ourselves." This ratio is explicated by two famous metaphors that he uses to describe the power of Fortune and the methods of checking it. The first of these may have been inspired by the regular flooding of the Arno, or perhaps by his disheartening experiences with the canal outside Pisa: "I compare Fortune to one of those violent rivers," he writes, "which, when they are enraged, flood the plains, tear down trees and buildings, wash soil from one place to deposit it in another." This destructive and seemingly unstoppable onrush may be opposed by such things as—and here speaks the veteran of hydraulic engineering projects— "constructing dykes and embankments so that when the river is in flood they would keep to one channel or their impetus will be less wild and dangerous." The course of a person's life, like the course of a river, may likewise be changed by means of ingenious and timely precautions.

Machiavelli's second metaphor alludes to the fact that Fortune was always seen as a feminine force. Like any woman, she responds best, he believes, to rough handling. He argues that in dealings with Fortune it is advisable to act impetuously "because Fortune is a woman and if she is to be submissive it is necessary to beat and coerce her." However disagreeable the image, it is worth remembering that gendered interpretations of philosophical conceptions have a lengthy history, and that Machiavelli elsewhere speaks of winning over Fortune by means of friendship and harmonious action. The idea of battering Fortune into submission did not, in fact, originate with Machiavelli. Seventy years earlier, in *Somnium de Fortuna* (The Dream of Fortune), Aeneas Silvius Piccolomini had Fortune claim she despised those who "run away from me" and favored "those who put me to flight." The upshot, at any rate, is that one can manage the caprice of Fortune—a comforting philosophy for the former Second Chancellor to contemplate from his lonely exile in the Albergaccio.

For Vettori, there could have been nothing especially objectionable—or especially original—in any of this. Machiavelli was employing a familiar humanist vocabulary to explore age-old concepts and philosophical questions. His arguments as well as his conclusions were similar to those of Petrarch, Piccolomini, and Pontano. But a crucial section of *The Prince* offered insights into governance that Vettori could have seen in none of these other works. This was his "original set of rules"—a topsy-turvy rendering of political morality that seems to have shocked Vettori into a prolonged and diffident silence.

The medieval "mirrors for princes" usually included sections on ethical behavior. In the first part of his *Government of Princes*, written about 1280, Giles of Rome, a pupil of Aquinas, had listed virtues for a ruler to practice and vices to avoid. His fairly predictable inventory included keeping oaths, observing laws, and showing mercy and magnanimity while shunning prodigality, avarice, and sundry other vices. Machiavelli, however, does not hold that this conventional morality is entirely practical in the brutal world of Italian politics. "The gulf between how one should live and how one does live is so wide," he writes, "that a man who neglects what is actually done for what should be done moves toward self-destruction rather than self-preservation." Nostrums having to do with keeping oaths and showing mercy are all very laudable on paper, but the man who transfers these moral precepts into the political arena will find himself drastically compromised. Machiavelli offers a new approach to political morality: "The fact is that a man who wants to act virtuously in every way necessarily comes to grief among so many who are not virtuous. Therefore if a prince wants to maintain his rule he must be prepared not to be virtuous, and to make use of this, or not, according to his need." Qualities that the world considers virtues will lead a leader to ruin, while those regarded as vices will often bring safety and prosperity. Good leadership requires a prince to "know how to do evil."

Machiavelli offers a number of examples to show how observing traditional ethical standards can doom a leader. Generosity may seem desirable in a prince, he observes, but reputations for munificence are achieved only through ostentatious expenditures that ultimately deplete a state's financial resources and lead to resentment and hatred. Miserliness, on the other hand, though commonly taken for a vice, can actually lead to the strengthening of the state. He gives as evidence the case of Louis XII of France, whose "long-standing parsimony" enabled him to keep taxes low despite having huge numbers of soldiers under arms.

A more disturbing example of Machiavelli's revision of political virtues and vices appears in Chapter 28, entitled "How Princes

Should Honor Their Word." Machiavelli admits that while it is commendable for a prince to keep his oaths and "to be straight-forward rather than crafty in his dealings," one cannot ignore the fact that a number of princes have achieved great successes by doing precisely the opposite. He specifically mentions Pope Alexander VI, but also prominent in his mind, no doubt, was Julius II, whom he had watched erase his promises with "the cotton-wool from the inkstand." Violating their oaths and knowing how to do evil, rather than exercising the cardinal virtues, had allowed these popes to accomplish their political objectives. Machiavelli does allow that a reputation for dishonesty can be detrimental to a leader. In 1505 he had lectured Gianpaolo Baglioni that by breaking his word to the Florentines he would be regarded by everyone as "a stumbling horse that nobody would ride for fear of getting his neck broken." To avoid invidious repute as an oath-breaker, an element of dissembling is therefore required. According to Machiavelli, a prince should not unswervingly practice honesty, compassion, and generosity, but he should merely *appear* to practice them, duping his subjects and allies into believing in his integrity while secretly performing his cunning intrigues.

Machiavelli's justification for tendering such unusual advice to princes is the moral deficiencies of their subjects, and of mankind in general. As a student of human nature, as a witness to much cruelty and cowardice, and as a victim of schemers and backbiters who had been cashiered from his position, wrongly implicated in a conspiracy, and then tortured in the Stinche, Machiavelli was more than a little cynical by the time he sat down to write in 1513. A prince needs to know how to do evil, he insists, for the simple reason that people themselves are evil. "One can make this generalization about men," he writes in one of the book's most misanthropic passages. "They are ungrateful, fickle liars and deceivers, they shun danger and are greedy for profit." Friendship "does not last and it yields nothing," while the bonds of love and gratitude are shattered whenever it is convenient or advantageous. In such a harsh and murky moral universe, what choice does a prince have but to act with equal brutality and faithlessness?

Another justification for such a chilling prescription is that it leads to worldly glory and the preservation of the state. Aquinas had claimed in *On Kingship* that these ends, however laudable in themselves, were always subservient to a higher goal, that is, eternal rewards in the afterlife, for the soul was more important than the state. Thus the Christian response to the sort of iniquitous behavior advocated in *The Prince* was the eternal damnation that awaited evil-doers: the wages of Guido da Montefeltro's breaking of oaths had been, according to Dante, a place in the Eighth Circle of Hell. Yet Machiavelli has nothing whatsoever to say about punishments in the afterlife. The cold-blooded and unashamed explication of "how to do evil" in the context of this blithe disregard for Christian doctrine was what would ultimately earn Machiavelli such a monstrous reputation. As the English historian Lord Macaulay would write in 1827, it was impossible to read *The Prince* without "horror and amazement." He claimed that "such a display of wickedness . . . such cool, judicious, scientific atrocity" appeared "rather to belong to a fiend than to the most depraved of men."

Francesco Vettori probably did not find the work as atrocious and depraved as so many later readers would. But he no doubt concluded that the more contentious claims in *The Prince* would do little to make its author welcome at the Medici court. This frank apologia for double-dealing and the divorce of politics from ethics would only have played into the hands of the enemies of the Medici regime, of whom there was no shortage in Florence by 1514. What could be more impolitic than offering a "handbook for tyrants"—as the book would soon come to be seen—to a member of the family that was trying to fend off a reputation as the thief of Florentine liberties?

Vettori urged his friend to forget his worldly aspirations and—ironically, given Machiavelli's argument in *The Prince*—to resign himself to the ruthless whimsy of Fortune. He himself claimed to have been reading Pontano's *On Fortune* and described its message (inaccurately) as one in which the author "clearly shows that neither talent, nor foresight, nor fortitude, nor the other virtues avail at all when Fortune is absent." Vettori clearly disagreed with the optimistic passages in *The Prince* about thrashing Fortune into submission. He thought his friend was sadly deluding himself if he believed he could stay her spinning wheel. There was nothing to do, he wrote to Machiavelli, but accept our lot, "and you especially . . . ought to do so."

Such advice was already superfluous. By the time Vettori wrote these words, Machiavelli had relinquished not only his hopes for a return to power but also his studies of the actions of men and their ways of doing things. "No longer," he wrote to

Vettori in the summer of 1514, "do I delight in reading about the deeds of the ancients or in discussing those of the moderns." Now, his efforts exhausted, Machiavelli, too, seemed to believe that not even the man of *virtù* could prevail once Fortune had turned her back on him.

Chapter Sixteen

THE REASON FOR Machiavelli's rejection of his studious life was not simply his disappointment at the reception of *The Prince*. The renunciation also had a happier cause: Machiavelli was in love. Fortune had finally smiled on him, he informed Francesco Vettori in the summer of 1514, "for while in the country I have met a creature so gracious, so refined, so noble—both in nature and in circumstance—that never could either my praise or my love for her be as much as she deserves."

The identity of this gracious and noble creature is not known for certain. It seems she was not a prostitute like La Riccia or Jeanne but rather an abandoned wife, the sister of a local man named Niccolò Tafani. Tafani's brother-in-law Giovanni had absconded to Rome with his wife's dowry, prompting Tafani to appeal to Machiavelli for assistance in tracking down the rogue. Machiavelli provided assistance by appealing in turn to

Vettori—and in the process found himself ensnared in "nets of gold woven by Venus." The affair brought him a rare peace of mind. Even though he had entered "a great travail," he nonetheless felt, he told Vettori, "a great sweetness in it, both because of the delight that rare and gentle countenance brings me and because I have laid aside all memory of my sorrows." There is no evidence how the anxious and volatile Marietta reacted to this latest dalliance on the part of her husband, if indeed she ever learned of it. But a dozen years of marriage must have accustomed her to the ways of a man addicted to "wandering and roaming about."

Machiavelli may have laid his sorrows aside, but he did not entirely forsake political discussion. In December he received a letter from Vettori soliciting his advice about how Leo X might best maintain the power and prestige of the Church in the current political climate. Should the pope ally himself with the French in their attempt to regain Milan, or were his interests better served by siding with the emperor and Spain? "Examine everything," Vettori instructed him. "I know you have such intelligence that although two years have gone by since you left the shop, I do not think you have forgotten the craft." Indeed he had not. Machiavelli responded with a 3,500-word letter in which he gave his friend the benefit of his considerable wisdom and experience. "For the past twenty years I do not think there has been a more serious problem than this one," he began before outlining the pros and cons of the various possible alliances and, in the end, arguing in favor of a French connection. Ten days later, not having received word back from Rome, he dispatched another 1,200 words on the subject. "You have stirred up my juices," he told Vettori.

Machiavelli's hopes were also stirring. He admitted to Vettori that if Fortune intended the Medici to employ him, "whether for affairs in Florence or abroad," he would finally be content. Vettori showed both letters—as Machiavelli no doubt hoped he would—to both Leo X and his cousin, Giulio de' Medici, the thirty-six-year-old Archbishop of Florence and a nephew of Lorenzo the Magnificent. The two men "were astonished at their wit and praised their judgment," according to Vettori, though "nothing else has been gotten from them but words." No offer of employment, that is, was forthcoming from the Vatican. The only thing that arrived from Rome, via Vettori, was a roll of blue yarn Machiavelli had ordered to make for a pair of stockings for his ladylove.

Hope sprang eternal, though. Early in 1515, another chink of light appeared thanks to Vettori's brother, Paolo. Since Leo X was determined to make Giuliano de' Medici ruler of the Romagna, and since Paolo Vettori was a good friend of Giuliano, it seemed certain that Paolo would be made the governor of one of the cities in the new princedom—in which case it seemed equally certain that something might finally be done for Machiavelli. Paolo and Machiavelli began meeting for discussions in Florence, with Machiavelli passing on advice about how the new principality should be ruled. He advised Paolo to follow the example of Cesare Borgia—"whose deeds I should imitate on all occasions"—and concentrate on unifying the Romagna into a single state. Paolo was impressed with this guidance, but

Machiavelli's hopes were thwarted when a proposal to take him into service was vetoed by none other than the Archbishop of Florence. Hearing of Paolo's plans to employ Machiavelli, the archbishop sternly informed the papal secretary "not to have anything to do with Niccolò." Machiavelli's advice may have been respected if not necessarily welcomed; but he was clearly not, in the eyes of the Medici, a man to be trusted.

"I have become useless to myself, to my family, and to my friends," Machiavelli wrote despondently to his nephew Giovanni some months later, "because my doleful fate has willed it to be so." Still, he absorbed this latest blow from Fortune and, like a true man of *virtù*, began thinking of other ways to counter his adversities. "I bide my time," he told Giovanni, "so that I may be ready to seize good Fortune should she come." Despite so many abrupt and obvious rebuffs, he still had not relinquished hopes for a Medici connection; and so sometime in the months that followed he turned his attention back to his little study of princes and principalities.

None of the Medici whom Machiavelli had been courting so assiduously—and so unsuccessfully—bore the least comparison to Lorenzo the Magnificent. Leo X had inherited his father's love of pageantry and luxury ("Let us enjoy the papacy since God has given it to us," he supposedly remarked after his election) but none of his aesthetic sensibility or diplomatic skills. Giuliano, suffering from syphilis, had singularly failed to accomplish anything noteworthy, while the archbishop, their cousin, though intelligent and industrious, was disastrously irresolute.

The dashed hopes for a return to the splendors of Lorenzo's reign received their tragic emblem at the end of 1515, when Leo returned to Florence for a visit amid elaborately staged celebrations. The festival included a symbol of the "Golden Age," a boy covered from head to toe in gold paint—which destroyed his skin and killed him three days later.

Possibly the most deficient member of the family was Lorenzo, son of the late Piero the Unfortunate. Lorenzo di Piero de' Medici had nothing in common with his illustrious grandfather except for his name. A portrait of Lorenzo carved by Michelangelo depicts the young man (born in 1492) as an exemplar of the contemplative life: dressed in the costume of an antique warrior, he sits in the New Sacristy in the church of San Lorenzo, lost in a philosophical daydream while the allegorical figures of Dawn and Dusk recline at his sandal-shod feet. Hardly could an image have offered a less reliable resemblance to its subject. Lorenzo was in fact an arrogant, inept, wayward, self-indulgent imbecile who had never enjoyed a moment's quiet, philosophical reflection in his life. Yet this is the buffoon on whom, by 1515, Machiavelli had fixed his hopes for advancement—as well as, apparently, his hopes for all of Italy.

Machiavelli had claimed to be impressed with the young Lorenzo de' Medici as early as 1514. "He has filled the entire city with high hopes," he wrote to Vettori, "and it seems that everyone is beginning to recognize in him the beloved memory of his grandfather." The compliment was a strange one. Machiavelli was one of the few people in Florence who held a favorable opinion of Lorenzo, who was actually doing the opposite of raising either high hopes or memories of his beloved grandfather. By 1514 he had already made himself deeply unpopular by never appearing in public except with an armed guard and by usurping for himself the powers of many civic officials. He also caused offense by wearing a Spanish-style beard and insisting that people should doff their hats before addressing him. So many complaints had been registered about his pompous and tyrannical behavior that his kinsman, the archbishop, wrote a stern letter urging him to accommodate himself to the wishes of the citizens.

The appeal fell on deaf ears. Despite his lack of success or experience on the battlefield, Lorenzo was named *Capitano della Guerra* in the spring of 1515, becoming the republic's military commander, complete with an exorbitant salary of 35,000 florins per year. Though he was supposed to take his orders from the Signoria, many in Florence felt he was now poised to assume absolute power. In any case, he was still putting on lordly airs and neglecting to consult the citizens. He made no secret, moreover, of the fact that he regarded Florence as a dull backwater in comparison to Rome and the court of Leo X. He openly coveted for himself the Duchy of Milan (a pipedream) and then (more realistically) that of Urbino. By early 1516 he had succeeded in alienating not only the common people but also the *ottimati*, many of whom had been Medici loyalists; and by April of that year he had become so loathsome that a hopeful rumor was making the rounds that the new King of France, François I, was preparing to invade Florence and restore both Piero Soderini and the Great Council of the People.

It was at this stangely inopportune moment that Machiavelli resolved to dedicate *The Prince* not to Giuliano de' Medici—who died from syphilis in March 1516—but to the despised and incompetent Lorenzo. Some time in the first half of 1516 he composed a letter of dedication to "Magnificent Lorenzo de' Medici" explaining how he hoped the young man would read and consider the treatise "diligently" in order to "reach the eminence that Fortune and your many qualities promise you." Requesting the diligent attentions of Lorenzo de' Medici was a sorry exercise in self-deception. Though accustomed to Medici rebuffs, Machiavelli was taken aback by a taste of the cavalier deliquency that had earned Lorenzo such a grotesque reputation. He happened to offer the treatise to Lorenzo at the same time as someone else gave His Magnificence a pair of hounds, for which Lorenzo supposedly expressed far more gratitude and enthusiasm. Machiavelli departed, according to legend, "in great indignation, telling his friends that he was not the man to conspire against princes, but that if they persisted in their ways conspiracies would surely occur." His words would prove to be prophetic.

Though still spending much of the year at his farm in Sant' Andrea in Percussina, by the summer of 1517 Machiavelli had more reason to pay regular visits to Florence. Much to his pleasure, he had become a member of a more lofty circle of intimates than the cardplayers in the tavern beside the Albergaccio.

For the past twenty-five years the gardens of the Palazzo Rucellai, near the Porta al Prato, had been the venue for the best intellectual and political discussions in Florence. For the past century the Rucellai had been one of Florence's wealthiest families. Their money as well as their name derived from a lichen called *orcella* or *roccella* that grew in Greece and the Canary Islands, and which one of their forebears, a cloth merchant, had turned into a purplish-red dye called *oricello*. Bernardo, who initiated the discussions, had used his share of the family fortune to collect antiquities, to decorate the façade of the church of Santa Maria Novella, and to win the hand of Lorenzo the Magnificent's sister, Nannina. After Lorenzo's death in 1492, the gardens of his palazzo hosted the Platonic Academy, the group of philosophers, poets, and humanists who had originally gathered outside Florence at the Villa di Careggi. After 1502 these gardens, known as the Orti Oricellari, had become the meeting place for the anti-Soderini faction. Bernardo Rucellai and his *ottimati* friends had been staunch Mediceans, with Bernardo helping to finance the Medici restoration in 1512 by loaning Giuliano the money with which to pay Ramón de Cardona.

For more than a decade, then, the Orti Oricellari would have been off-limits—and indeed repugnant—to Piero Soderini's *mannerino*. But after Bernardo's death in 1514, and after Lorenzo de' Medici proceeded to sabotage his popularity with authoritarian behavior, the political temper of many of the denizens of the Orti Oricellari changed. By the time Machiavelli became a regular visitor in 1517, the Orti Oricellari was a hotbed of anti-Medici dissent—though it should be noted that several members, such as Filippo de' Nerli, a member of the Signoria in 1517, remained staunch Mediceans. Nonetheless, Machiavelli's appearance among the antique statues and manicured groves of the Palazzo Rucellai signaled not only his desire for intellectual companionship but also his growing disenchantment with the Medici regime.

Machiavelli certainly found intellectual companionship among the young men in the Orti Oricellari. He called these fellow habitués his "noontime friends"—as opposed, perhaps, to his "midnight friends," the cronies with whom he gambled and the prostitutes with whom he consorted. The Orti Oricellari provided the philosophical stimulation and bonhomous social interaction he had been lacking since his removal from office five years earlier. The host was Cosimo Rucellai, Bernardo's nephew, a young man so badly crippled from gout and assailed by syphilis that he was carried into the gardens to preside over the discussions—which he seems to have done with wit and grace—from a bed shaped like a cradle. Other members included a twenty-three-year-old biblical scholar named Antonio Brucioli (whose translations of the Old and New Testaments would much later attract the attentions of the Inquisition) and a forty-one-year-old playwright and former follower of Savonarola (and future historian of Florence) named Jacopo Nardi. The members to whom Machiavelli became closest, besides Cosimo, seem to have been Luigi Alamanni, a well-known poet, and Zanobi Buondelmonti, a young man from an ancient Florentine family. They came together primarily to discuss philosophy, history, literature, and statecraft. However, since Nardi, like Machiavelli, was a composer of carnival songs, no doubt moments were devoted to the strumming of rebecs and the venting of high spirits in song.

While the Medici spurned Machiavelli's political reflections and advice, the members of the Orti Oricellari were eager to hear him speak. Soon after joining he began reading to them passages from a treatise he had been composing sporadically for the previous four or five years, a commentary on a book he knew and greatly admired, Livy's *History of Rome*—the same work his father, Bernardo, had acquired in 1475 by compiling an index of place names for the printer. Livy's magnum opus, begun about 29 B.C., stretched to 142 books (of which only thirty-five survive) and covered the entire history of ancient Rome, from its founding after the fall of Troy. Yet it is not merely a straightforward chronicle of events. Its opening premise is that, as Livy writes in his prologue, "no country has ever been greater or purer than ours or richer in good citizens and noble deeds." Livy also claims in his prologue that the study of history "is the best medicine for a sick mind" because it can provide "both examples and warnings: fine things to take as models, base things, rotten through and through, to avoid."

Machiavelli concurred with Livy on both counts. He turned to Livy's narrative of Rome's illustrious history for the political lessons that could be drawn from it and then applied them to the ailing body politic of present-day Florence. If the reasons behind the success of the Roman Republic could be properly understood, then these ancient triumphs might be repeated. If *The Prince* was about how to gain, rule, and maintain a principality, then this new work—entitled *Discourses on the First Ten*

Decades of Livy—concerned itself with how to establish and maintain a healthy republic. Machiavelli was still examining the mechanics of power, but this time from the perspective of a popular rather than a princely government. Five years of oligarchic Medicean rule in Florence had apparently made him nostalgic, like his friends in the Orti Oricellari, for a purer, republican form of government.

Machiavelli's overarching preoccupation in the *Discourses* is political liberty. Since he argues that cities flourish economically and militarily only if they enjoy a popular government, the question obviously arises as to how such liberty can be acquired and maintained. Livy himself believed the good offices of Fortune were almost always involved, but Machiavelli stresses that liberty vitally depends on the *virtù* of the population. The example of the Roman Republic reveals that the self-interest of individuals must be put aside in favor of a patriotic commitment to the greater good. But how can such *virtù* and patriotism be fostered in a city's population, he wonders, given that, as he writes in a grim echo of *The Prince*, most people "are more prone to evil than to good"?[1]

To answer this vexing question, Machiavelli turns to a close study of the history and institutions of the Roman Republic. He observes the part played by good leadership, coercive laws, an inspiring religion (he particularly admires the Romans' solemn oaths and bloody sacrifices), and a mixed government that included both the nobles and the plebeians. Throughout his long discussion, the praise of ancient Rome is shot through with a lament for its lost glories and a horror of the state of affairs—

corruption, servitude, military incompetence—in contemporary Italy. Florence comes in for particularly pointed criticism. According to Machiavelli, the city was doomed from the start. In the very first chapter of Book I he dourly remarks that cities founded by others (and Florence was established, he notes, by the Imperial Romans) "rarely make great progress" and therefore cannot ever be "numbered among the chief kingdoms." Elsewhere in the *Discourses* he argues that cities beginning life in this state of servility to another power will find it "not merely difficult but impossible" to find ways of acquiring and then preserving their freedom. Florence's greatness and liberty were, in effect, smothered in the cradle.

The concern in the *Discourses* with popular rather than princely government—with government by the many rather than the few—must have come as a surprise to those in the Orti Oricellari who knew Machiavelli as the author of *The Prince*. Yet there is still much in the treatise that would have sounded familiar to readers of his earlier work. Machiavelli praises the use of deceit in warfare, pointing out that however detestable dishonesty might seem, "nevertheless in war it is praiseworthy and brings fame." Another familiar lesson appears when he writes about the extreme measures that must be taken to preserve a republic from its enemies: "When it is absolutely a question of the safety of one's country, there must be no consideration of what is just or unjust, of merciful or cruel, of praiseworthy or disgraceful." The only relevant consideration is what will save the state and maintain its liberty. His view in this matter was no doubt colored by what had transpired in

Florence under Piero Soderini in 1512, since he disapproves of how Soderini depended upon his "patience and goodness" and respect for the laws rather than taking extraordinary measures—even violent and oppressive ones—both to save himself and to safeguard Florence against the Medici.

Machiavelli's auditors in the Orti Oricellari could not fail to have been impressed with the *Discourses*. It is an undeniably brilliant work, moving with smooth self-assurance from microscopic scrutiny to panoramic survey. Erudite, provocative, and ambitious, and composed in Machiavelli's well-honed prose, it aims at nothing less than an explication of the general laws of statecraft. It pursues this goal, among other ways, by announcing hypotheses he then proceeds to test—thereby offering an early example of the style of inductive reasoning that was soon to underpin the scientific method. Even more than *The Prince*, it gives testimony to how Machiavelli had, for fifteen years of government service, made an acute and unceasing study of the art of the state.

Yet, despite the shrewd observations and adroit arguments, there is a strange contradiction at the heart of the entire project. Machiavelli states in the prologue to Book I that he wants his readers to join him in a diligent study of the past and to imitate the best examples of the ancients. Imitation is possible, he assures us, because human nature, like the motion of the sun or the composition of the elements, is the same across the centuries; and it is therefore theoretically possible for Italians of the sixteenth century to behave in exactly the same way—with exactly the same patriotism and *virtù*—as the ancients. However, imitation presupposes conscious choice, and Machiavelli is in fact deeply skeptical about whether or not men have any freedom to choose the way they act.

The crucial passage comes in Book III, chapter 9, titled "How One Must Change with the Times If He Wants to Have Good Fortune Always." The theme of changing with the times is familiar from *The Prince*, where success comes to the person "who adapts his policy to the times." But here in the *Discourses* Machiavelli's argument echoes more resoundingly his observations to Giovan Battista Soderini about the actions of men and their ways of doing things. "I have many times considered," he writes, "that the causes of the good and bad fortunes of men depend on the manner of their proceeding with the times." Some men, he believes, proceed with "drive," others with "consideration and caution." Both methods may meet with success depending on that all-important variable—the specific historical circumstances. The trick is knowing when to proceed impulsively and when to employ consideration and caution.

As in the case of his 1506 letter to Giovan Battista, though, Machiavelli is deeply pessimistic about anyone ever actually being able to make this choice. He offers two recent cases, those of Piero Soderini and of Julius II. The former, he points out, proceeded with "kindness and patience" in all his affairs (a claim that may have raised the eyebrows of the Pisans, who starved during Soderini's blockade of their city in 1509). He prospered while the times were favorable to this policy, "but when afterward the times came in which he needed to break off his patience and humility, he could not do it. Hence, along with his city, he fell." Julius II, on the other hand, proceeded with "haste and vehemence," finding success in his enterprises because the times accorded with this kind of behavior. But had the times required patience and humility, "of necessity he would have fallen, because he would not have changed either his method or his rule of action."

The reason why neither Soderini nor Julius could change his manner or conduct was twofold. In the first place, someone who has achieved great success by behaving impetuously will find it difficult to heed the counsel of those warning him to act differently. But there is also a more formidable impediment: the fact that, as Machiavelli writes, "we cannot resist that to which nature inclines us." This law of necessity means Julius will always behave with impetuosity and fury, Soderini invariably with patience and humility. It is quite simply impossible for either of them to act otherwise—for Soderini to act like Julius, or vice versa. As Machiavelli had expressed the problem to Giovan Battista Soderini in 1506: "Men are unable to master their own natures." Far from being able to learn from history and wisely adapt themselves according to the temper of the times, rulers are powerless to change their ways of proceeding.

This pessimistic argument about human nature is an odd one for Machiavelli to make, as it seems to do away with the whole point of treatises like *The Prince* and the *Discourses*. These works are meant to offer political prescriptions to leaders, to show them how they must find success by altering their directions and ideas. Yet Machiavelli argues that no one can possibly make this vital switch: all men are passive reagents to their own natures. But if a prince cannot change his nature and thereby his way of acting—if he has no choice in his political decisions—then what is the purpose of spilling so much ink dispensing wisdom and advice? Machiavelli's writings presuppose, on the one hand, that men have freedom of action and that the study of history will teach them the best policy; on the other hand, he denies them this freedom, making them the helpless playthings of their own natures, inevitably doomed to failure once they are out of joint with the times.

Machiavelli's *Discourses* are likewise extremely dubious about man's ability to counter Fortune. In *The Prince* he had written that it was possible to oppose Fortune through the exercise of *virtù*. Yet by the time he comes to write the *Discourses*, Fortune apparently brooks no opposition. The twenty-ninth chapter of Book II is forbiddingly (and prolixly) entitled "Fortune Blinds the Intellects of Men When She Does Not Want Them to Oppose Her Plans." Here he announces that "men are able to assist Fortune but cannot thwart her. They can weave her designs but not destroy them." This is not quite a prescription for despair, though, since he writes that men can always hope that Fortune, who "goes through crooked and unknown roads," will one day favor them. The dynamic man of *virtù* from *The Prince*, raising defenses against Fortune and pummeling her with his fists, has become in the *Discourses* someone whose sole recourse is to wait and hope. In these rather dispiriting lines we glimpse the dejected man in the Albergaccio anxiously awaiting the call that never comes.

Chapter Seventeen

MACHIAVELLI WROTE A long letter at the end of 1517 to a friend from the Orti Oricellari, twenty-three-year-old Luigi Alamanni, who recently had gone to Rome. He told Alamanni how he was reading Ludovico Ariosto's epic poem *Orlando Furioso*, the first forty cantos of which had been published in the spring of 1516. Machiavelli had probably met Ariosto, the court poet of Ferrara, several years earlier, either at Rome or, more likely, in Florence, since Ariosto had arrived in Florence for a six-month sojourn in March 1513. During that period the poet stayed in an old Knights of Malta hospice on the south end of the Ponte Vecchio, only a matter of yards from Machiavelli's house.

Machiavelli was full of praise for Ariosto's work. "The entire poem is really fine and many passages are marvelous," he informed Alamanni, asking him to pass along his compliments to the author. He did, however, have one minor complaint.

Ariosto's sprawling poem celebrates a number of contemporary painters—including Michelangelo ("more divine than human"), Leonardo, Raphael, and Titian—as well as poets and writers such as Pietro Bembo, Baldassare Castiglione, and even Luigi Alamanni himself.[1] Nowhere, though, was there mention of Machiavelli's name. Machiavelli was miffed—or pretended to be miffed—at this glaring omission. "In his mention of so many poets," he wrote to Alamanni, "like some prick, he has left me out."

Ariosto may well have been surprised that Machiavelli considered himself a poet. He must also have been unconvinced by the claim, since his subsequent revisions to and enlargements of the 300,000-word poem (new editions would appear in 1521 and 1532) found no room in its roll call of Italy's illustrious poets for Machiavelli's name. Nonetheless, by 1517, as his hopes for advancement under the Medici receded, Machiavelli was nursing literary ambitions, writing not only poetry but also a novella and several plays. It constituted a remarkably prolific literary output at a time when he was in all probability putting the finishing touches on the *Discourses*.

Machiavelli's first visits to the Orti Oricellari had coincided with his efforts on a comic poem entitled *The Ass* (often erroneously called *The Golden Ass*) that he ambitiously composed in terza rima, the verse form of Dante's *Divine Comedy*. The satirical work was inspired in part by Lucius Apuleius's *The Golden Ass*, a bawdy Latin novel about a young man whose obsessive interest in magic gets him metamorphosed into an ass, and in part by myths about Circe, the enchantress who turned men into beasts. Machiavelli may well have read passages from *The Ass* to his friends in the Orti Oricellari. If so, the poem would have had a familiar ring to those who had also listened to his *Discourses*.

The Ass begins with Machiavelli turning his self-pity about his unfortunate situation into a comic persona. In the opening lines the poem's narrator compares himself to the ass about which he sings, pointing out that he is accustomed to slander and ingratitude, and that he expects "no pay, reward, or recompense" for his efforts. He then offers a curious but revealing parable, the story of a young Florentine who suffered from a peculiar ailment, "namely, that in every place he went running through the street, and at every time, without heed." The boy's concerned father consulted numerous wise men, who suggested the application of various remedies, all to no avail. Finally, a quack doctor began treating the youth, bleeding him and holding various perfumes under his nose. The quack also recommended a strict regimen whereby the young man was never allowed into the street unaccompanied or unrestrained. The treatment seemed to be taking effect, until one day the patient was allowed outdoors with his two brothers. When he reached the Via de' Martelli, from which he could see the broad and tempting stretch of the Via Larga, "his hair began to stand on end. Nor could this youth restrain himself, when he saw this street so straight and wide, from turning again to his old pleasure."

As the boy sprints heedlessly down the Via Larga, the lesson of the story is made clear to Machiavelli's readers: "The mind of man, ever intent on what is natural to it, grants no protection against either habit or nature." It is the same lesson in determinism that had been offered, years earlier, to Giovan Battista Soderini, and then emphasized in the *Discourses*.

Machiavelli ultimately left the poem unfinished, and in its unpolished state it hardly qualifies for praise by Ariosto. But the poem is notable for its bleak and rueful observations on the human condition. Philosophers and theologians had usually insisted on a firm distinction between men and beasts. Dante joined a longstanding tradition when he argued, in Book III of *Il Convivio*, that the rational soul was unique to human beings. Most writers accepted that higher reason made man suppress his animal instincts and participate in the divine. According to Dante, "Man is therefore called by the philosophers the Divine Animal." But for Machiavelli there is nothing divine about the human animal, a creature who (as a pig informs the narrator) is more vulnerable and pitiable—and more the sport of Fortune—than any beast. The bestial transformation in *The Ass* is a metaphor for the argument, familiar from the *Discourses*, that man can never escape his natural condition.

Possibly around this same time (the precise date is not actually known) Machiavelli also composed another work, a 3,000-word novella, *The Fable of Belfagor*. Another satirical story of transformation, it describes how a devil named Belfagor was sent to earth by Pluto to investigate whether wives were the cause of all earthly misfortune, as the men in the Underworld claimed. The tale is perhaps less interesting for its literary qualities than for what it suggests about Machiavelli's relations with Marietta and his opinions regarding marriage in general. Released from the Underworld, Belfagor goes to Florence, marries a noblewoman named Onesta, and soon finds himself bankrupted by her extravagance. He flees his creditors and falls in with Gianmatteo, a peasant who hides him from his pursuers in a dunghill. After a series of tricks and adventures, Belfagor flees back to the Underworld when he himself is tricked into thinking Onesta has come to fetch him back. He prefers the torments of Hell to the "annoyance, anxiety, and danger" of the "marriage yoke."

A somewhat more optimistic view of marriage and human relationships is found in a five-act play called *The Woman from Andros* that Machiavelli wrote late in 1517 or early 1518. Not exactly an original composition, the comedy is a translation, albeit with much reworking and updating, of a play of the same name by the Roman dramatist Terence. The work follows a time-honored comic pattern: a lovesick young man (Panfilo) hopes to marry a young woman despite the opposition of his father, and he succeeds thanks to an unexpected plot twist that reveals the true identity of his beloved. Due to its Roman source, the comedy features a number of themes at surprising variance with advice offered in *The Prince*. It emphasizes, for example, the importance of keeping vows: the suitor Panfilo prevails by keeping his promises to his beloved as well as to his father. Even more interesting is the fact that the play demonstrates the futility of schemes and underhanded stratagems when the machinations of a slave named Davo—described as a *ribaldo*—come to nothing. Deceit is shown to fail whereas honesty brings rewards and happiness. The shortcomings of Davo's schemes are intriguing in the context of the comic tradition, since he is a stock character known as the *dolosus servus*, the tricky slave, an agent who typically hatches the schemes that bring about the hero's success and happiness.

Schemes and stratagems pay better dividends in another comedy composed by Machiavelli in 1518. Unlike *The Woman from Andros*, this five-act play, *La Mandragola* (The Mandrake) was a completely original work in which Machiavelli gave free rein to his rapier wit and lascivious imagination. It begins with the same convention inherited from Roman comedy: a young man (Callimaco) desires a beautiful young woman (Lucrezia) but is faced with an impediment—though this time the hindrance to the lovers is not a disapproving father but rather the lady's husband, a doltish lawyer, as well as her own virtue. The fact that Callimaco's happiness can only be obtained through an act of adultery suggests a rather darker moral universe than that of *The Woman of Andros*. However, in the prologue Machiavelli explains that if such material seems unworthy or unsuitable, then the audience should bear in mind the unhappy situation of the author. The enforced retirement at Sant' Andrea in Percussina is once more lamented as Machiavelli describes himself as a man who has been

> . . . reduced to indolence
> And has no other way to turn,
> Condemned to an enforced sojourn,
> All worthwhile occupations barred
> Or, at the least, denied reward.[2]

The play also includes a bitter diatribe against the corruption and injustices of Florence, a city where, as one character observes, "there's nothing but a bunch of shit-asses," and where "anybody who doesn't have connections . . . is lucky if he can get the time of day." Though these words are put into the mouth of Nicia, the foolish old husband, there can be little doubt they mirror Machiavelli's own disenchantment with how his tireless efforts had been rewarded with ingratitude and contempt.

La Mandragola has for its plot an elaborate practical joke. Callimaco is convinced by his friend Ligurio, a former marriage-broker, that he can trick Nicia into allowing Callimaco to bed Lucrezia. The stratagem involves Callimaco posing as a doctor and offering Nicia, who desperately wants an heir, a potion guaranteed to get Lucrezia pregnant. This potion is made from the root of a mandrake, a plant more usually associated with sickness and death (the Latin *mandragora* means "harmful to cattle") rather than fertility. There were numerous legends about the plant, one of which was that it grew under the gallows where murderers were hung. Anyone who dared dig up the plant, according to another legend, would die soon afterward, and so in order to uproot a mandrake it was necessary to tie a dog to the plant: the animal would duly extract the root and expire.

Machiavelli was clearly familiar with these legends, since the mandrake potion offered to Nicia has a serious drawback: the person who sleeps with Lucrezia after she has taken the potion will die within the week. There is an antidote, however. Callimaco tells Nicia that—rather like the dog sacrificed to harvest the mandrake—someone else can be used to draw off the poison. This expediency will enable Callimaco to sleep with Lucrezia, but first Nicia and then (more problematically) Lucrezia must be convinced to sacrifice the life of a supposedly unwitting victim (Callimaco) for the sake of conceiving a child. Nicia is persuaded easily enough, but in order to acquire Lucrezia's consent both her mother and a corrupt priest, Friar Timoteo, are enlisted. Lucrezia eventually submits, downs the potion, and sleeps with Callimaco. Learning the full details of the scheme from Callimaco's postcoital confession, she decides that "divine providence has willed it so" and—here is the happy ending—agrees to continue sleeping with Callimaco until old Nicia finally dies and the two of them can be married.

The play is full of wonderful low comedy. Nicia is a particularly fine creation, a pompous old lawyer whose gullibility makes him a willing cuckold. There are nice comic set pieces, such as the presentation onstage of a urine sample and Nicia's description of how he closely examined Callimaco's genitalia for signs of the pox before he allowed him to sleep with his wife. The play is equally successful with its racy vernacular language. Machiavelli's barnyard vocabulary supplies a stream of exclamations such as *caccasangue* (literally, "bloody shit") and *caccastecche* ("shit-sticks").

The play is notable most of all for both its satire on the clergy and its portrayal of how ends can be achieved by the most unscrupulous of means. "We must always consider whether the end justifies the means," Friar Timoteo tells Lucrezia as he tries to persuade her to break her marriage vows and bring about someone else's untimely death. Like Machiavelli in *The Prince*, the friar complicates the relationship between virtue and vice, arguing that conventional ethical standards do not always hold. It is important to note that because the friar's argument is conducted with no lack of sophistry—and because he is motivated solely by the prospect of financial gain—Machiavelli is offering a parody not only of a corrupt priesthood but also, very possibly, of the arguments advanced in *The Prince*. Or, at the very least, he is suggesting that the frauds acceptable in the political arena are not quite so unobjectionable when it comes to the bedroom.

La Mandragola was finished in 1518 or, at the latest, in 1519. Machiavelli's expectations for the play were probably relatively modest. No public theaters were to be found in Florence (or anywhere in Italy) at this time. Scripted comedies were still peripheral cultural events compared to, say, the popular folk dramas performed in the piazzas during Carnival. Italian drama consisted in the main of what was known as *commedia erudita*—"erudite," or "scholarly," comedy based on the works of the Roman dramatists Plautus and Terence and performed in Latin at the universities and schools. Recently, though, a handful of writers had begun adapting these original sources—as Machiavelli had done with *The Woman from Andros*—in the Italian vernacular, with present-day settings and modern characters. The court at Ferrara had staged Ariosto's *La Cassaria*, based on Plautine models, in 1508, and then a second play,

The Pretenders, in 1509. A few years later, in 1513, Bernardo Dovizi da Bibbiena's *La Calandra*, likewise drawn from a play by Plautus, was presented to the court at Urbino during Carnival celebrations. But these sorts of plays, however amusing and intellectually accessible, were performed by amateur actors (that sometimes included children) before small aristocratic audiences, usually at court—even at the Vatican following Leo X's election. They were often presented merely as part of a larger spectacle: *The Pretenders*, for example, appeared on a bill that included both musical entertainment and a performance of mime and dancing called a *moresca*. An even more select audience had watched a play by Machiavelli's friend Jacopo Nardi in 1512: *The Comedy of Friendship*, a dramatization of a story from Boccaccio's *Decameron*, was staged for members of the Signoria.

Fame and Fortune, in short, did not appear to crook their fingers at a writer of comedies, though Machiavelli may have noted how well-wrought plays such as those by his friend Ariosto were a means of ingratiating oneself to a powerful patron. In any case, *La Mandragola* went into rehearsals with actors of the Orti Oricellari in the early weeks of 1520. It received its first performance during Carnival, in February of that year. Virtually nothing else is known about this production, though the play was probably presented to a restricted audience in the open-air of the Orti Oricellari, with amateur actors, musical interludes, and a painted backcloth along the lines of the cityscape of Ferrara (painted, according to legend, by Raphael) that had served *The Pretenders*. By that time, one of Callimaco's lines in the play's opening scene—"Nothing is ever so desperate that there is no ground for hope"—seemed very appropriate. For, at the dawn of this new decade, Machiavelli suddenly appeared to have grounds to hope for a change of luck.

Machiavelli's fortunes began to improve only after the death of the man to whom he had dedicated *The Prince.* Lorenzo di Piero de' Medici died of syphilis in May 1519, at the age of twenty-six. The city's affairs were thereafter directed by Giulio de' Medici, the Archbishop of Florence. Though earlier he had warned his underlings "not to have anything to do with Niccolò," by early 1520 the archbishop had qualified his position. Thanks to the intervention of Lorenzo Strozzi, a member of the Orti Oricellari, he met with Machiavelli in the middle of March 1520, a month after the first performance of *La Mandragola.*

The archbishop was canvassing widely for opinions about how the government of Florence should be run, and it was probably at this meeting that he commissioned from Machiavelli a study that became *Discourse on Florentine Affairs After the Death of Lorenzo.* This treatise, composed sometime in 1520, included a blueprint for government that would safeguard the Republic but also enshrine Medici dominance. Machiavelli's proposal recommended such measures as bringing back both the Great Council of the People and the Gonfalonier for Life. There was little chance of the archbishop agreeing to these terms—but at least Machiavelli was once more involved, however remotely, in affairs of government.

A month after his meeting with the archbishop, Machiavelli received further encouraging news. At the end of April 1520, Battista della Palla, a fellow member of the Orti Oricellari, gave a pulse-quickening account to Machiavelli of his meeting in Rome with Pope Leo X. "I have spoken of your affairs in detail with the pope," he told Machiavelli, "and in truth, as far as can be seen, I have found him very well disposed toward you." He claimed the pope had a mind to commission Machiavelli "to do some writing or something else." His Holiness was a worldly man who loved the theater. In 1514 he had ordered a performance in Rome of Bibbiena's *La Calandra*, and now he was interested in *La Mandragola*. It seems that after Leo learned of the play's great success in Florence (possibly from his cousin, the archbishop) he demanded that it be staged at the papal court with the same actors and scenery. "I think it is going to give him great pleasure," predicted della Palla.

The command performance duly took place later that same year, repeating its Florentine success. That the pope could laugh at a play featuring a venal priest is admirable considering how around this same time, in June 1520, he excommunicated Martin Luther, the man whose ninety-five theses had attacked, among other things, the "lust and license" of the clergy. In any case, *La Mandragola* more than anything else turned out to be the key to Machiavelli's return into the good graces of the Medici. An off-color drama of bed-hopping, chicanery, and ecclesiastical corruption succeeded where *The Prince* had failed.

Machiavelli had loftier plans for his literary career than *La Mandragola*. The opportunity "to do some writing" for the

Medici seems to have bent his thoughts toward composing a history of Florence, a major project he hoped might be funded by the Medici. The chance to advertise his services came in the summer of 1520, when he was sent to Lucca to pressure a bankrupt Lucchese merchant to pay his debts. It was a modest task for a man who had traveled four times to the court of Louis XII, but a short spell of leisure in Lucca provided Machiavelli with the occasion for a dress rehearsal, so to speak, for a larger historical work. In the space of a few weeks he composed *The Life of Castruccio Castracani*, a 10,000-word biography of a red-haired, fourteenth-century Lucca-born *condottiere* who had defeated the Florentines in 1325.

The Life of Castruccio Castracani is an amusing read, full of anecdote and incident. However, it was not altogether the best example of Machiavelli's skills as a historian. Myth and invention are grafted rather obviously onto the framework of Castruccio's life, the dates and facts of which get carefree treatment. Machiavelli invents, for example, the fact that Castruccio (whose surname means "castrator of dogs") was a foundling—a contrivance supposedly serving to show how all great men have been born in obscurity or have "suffered to an unusual degree from the travails of Fortune."[3] Many of Machiavelli's hobby-horses can be found in the work, from the malice of Fortune (Castruccio is given a dying speech in which he acknowledges Fortune and not *virtù* to be supreme in human affairs) to the need for a strong and resolute leader. There is also praise for Castruccio's "beautiful deceptions," such as the time he solved problems of factional strife in Pistoia (the city whose feuds had so frustrated Machiavelli in 1501) by befriending each side and then mercilessly slaughtering both.

At the end of summer Machiavelli sent a manuscript of the work to his friends Zanobi Buondelmonti and Luigi Alamanni (Cosimo Rucellai had died a year earlier). Zanobi wrote back with high praise, reporting that the work had been "universally commended" by the members of the Orti Oricellari—though he pointed out that some sections "could nonetheless be improved," in particular by the removal of the maxims that Machiavelli had cribbed from writers such as Diogenes Laertius and wrongly attributed to Castruccio. Still, Zanobi ventured that this "model of a history" revealed Machiavelli's suitability for beginning the much grander project of a history of Florence.

This project came to fruition soon afterward. Machiavelli returned from Lucca in mid-September, and two months later he received a commission from Leo X and the archbishop to compose a new history of Florence. His contract stated that he should write the history of the city of Florence, "from whatever time seems most suitable to him, and in whatever language—either Latin or Tuscan—may seem best to him." His payment was to be one hundred florins, a sum that was twenty-eight florins less than his annual salary as Second Chancellor. However, the comparatively small remuneration was offset by the prestige of the commission. Not only did it come from the pope, but it placed Machiavelli in the tradition of the Florentine Republic's chroniclers and historians, celebrated men such as Poggio Bracciolini and Leonardo Bruni, the latter of whom had received a lifetime's tax exemption for himself and his children as gratitude for his twelve-book *History of the Florentine People*, written in the 1420s.

Machiavelli immediately set to work, using for references those works and others, including Flavio Biondo's *Decades of History from the Decline of the Roman Empire*, a book purchased by his father in 1485. He also used a chronicle of Florence written by Piero Minerbetti. In the front of this latter work he composed a short verse: "O Machiavelli, who amuse yourself with me / Be careful not to touch me with the lamp / Give me back soon, and keep me away from children." These lighthearted and amusing lines testify to a brightening of Machiavelli's dark mood. After eight years of trying, he had at long last entered the service of the Medici.

Chapter Eighteen

MACHIAVELLI'S WORK ON his history of Florence was interrupted in the spring of 1521 when, as in the old days, he climbed into the saddle and rode off on government business. The board in charge of Florence's foreign affairs, the Otto di Pratica, had selected him to travel sixty miles north to the city of Carpi, where the friars of the Franciscan Order were holding their general chapter. Though the Franciscan Order had recently been reformed, some of the friars in Florence had evidently fallen short of the piety and restraint outlined in the Rule of Saint Francis. Finding some of the friars badly behaved, the Otto di Pratica was determined to stamp out their offenses by exercising a more rigid control over the friaries lying within Florentine territories. Machiavelli was the improbable emissary dispatched to conduct these negotiations.

The strange incongruity of the scandalous habitué of Florence's whorehouses lecturing Franciscans about lapses in morality was not lost on Machiavelli, who regarded with some levity his mission to what he derided as the "Republic of Clogs." For their part, the friars must have been surprised when the ambassador from Florence appearing in their midst turned out to be the priest-gobbling author of *La Mandragola*. Predictably, events over the next few days degenerated to the level of farce as Machiavelli began making mischief among his baffled hosts. Bored by having to wait while the Franciscans selected their officials, he began contemplating ways in which to (as he put it in a letter to a friend) "stir up such strife among them . . . that they might start going after one another with their wooden clogs." He soon involved this friend, Francesco Guicciardini, the governor of nearby Modena, in a practical joke that saw Guicciardini dispatching a succession of messengers to Machiavelli's residence in Carpi. The messengers were to arrive galloping full tilt and bearing what appeared to be important documents; these were meant to impress the friars with Machiavelli's involvement in weighty affairs. The trick began to misfire, however, when Machiavelli's host, a member of the Chancellery in Carpi named Gismondo Santi, grew suspicious. Machiavelli had been enjoying a lavish hospitality in Gismondo's quarters, with "splendid beds" and enough food at each meal "for six dogs and three wolves." He became concerned that Gismondo, feeling he had been made a fool of, might pack him off to the more modest pleasures of a local inn. The jape ended with Machiavelli writing a desperate plea to Guicciardini to call off the galloping messengers.

Machiavelli also had a second assignment at Carpi. He had

been charged by the consuls of the Wool Guild with the task of finding a preacher for the Lenten sermons; in particular, the consuls wished him to secure the services of a Franciscan by the name of Giovanni Gualberto da Firenze, also known as "Il Rovaio" (which was the name of a cold northerly wind and therefore probably testifies to Brother Giovanni's scathing style of preaching). Guicciardini found his friend's task a delightfully incongruous one that was akin, he told Machiavelli, to having a notorious Florentine sodomite named Pacchierotto trying to find someone a wife. As for Il Rovaio himself—"that traitor Rovaio," as Machiavelli called him—he was in no hurry to go to Florence since he complained that his words were little heeded there. He had already preached sermons in Florence in which he ordered all prostitutes to wear yellow veils, yet he had recently received word from his sister, he indignantly informed Machiavelli, that the whores in Florence "appear as they please and wiggle their tails more than ever." It was no doubt a relief for Machiavelli when, at the end of the month, he was back in the Albergaccio, among his books and papers.

Machiavelli's trip to Carpi and his handling of the Franciscans raise the question of his views on religion in general and on Christianity in particular. Guicciardini had jokingly warned Machiavelli that he must not spend too long in Carpi lest "those holy friars might pass some of their hypocrisy on to you"; and he noted that if Machiavelli suddenly turned religious it would be attributed "rather to senility than to goodness" because "you have always lived in a contrary belief." Machiavelli was certainly not opposed to religion, but for him it possessed only an instrumental value: he was not interested in what religion could do for the soul in the afterlife, only in what benefits it might have for society in the here-and-now. The ancient Romans had used oaths and other religious rites, he noted approvingly in the *Discourses*, to inspire their citizens to accomplish heroic deeds and thereby to preserve and protect the republic. But he was much less convinced about the potential for Christianity to achieve similar ends. In the *Discourses* he complained that his contemporaries in Christian Europe were less brave and ferocious than the ancient Romans because of the enervating effects of the Christian religion. For while the ancient Romans had esteemed the honors of the world and performed bloody sacrifices—acts that Machiavelli believed motivated them in battle—present-day Christianity featured neither blood rites nor esteem for earthly glory. Christianity, he lamented, acclaimed humble and contemplative men rather than men of action.

This analysis conveniently ignored brawnier versions of Christianity such as the Crusades or, more recently, the military campaigns of Julius II, which had witnessed the pope marching behind the consecrated Host. But it reflects Machiavelli's very real disappointment that Christian Europe had failed to emulate the civic and political standards of ancient Rome. It also reflects the widespread disenchantment with the hypocrisy and corruption of the Church and some of the religious orders—a disenchantment that underpinned not only the sharp satirical bite of *La Mandragola* but also the castigations of ecclesiastical corruption in Martin Luther's ninety-five theses. Coincidently, Machiavelli's embassy to the "Republic of Clogs" took place against the background of momentous events occurring in the Rhineland city of Worms, where in May the new Holy Roman Emperor, Charles V, imposed an imperial edict against Luther, banning his books and declaring him an outlaw. There is a world of difference between the philosophies of Machiavelli and Luther, the latter of whom urged his followers to seek a place in heaven by means of the kind of life of humility and inner repentance that so repelled Machiavelli. But both men believed, on the basis of similar observations, that Christianity had taken some disastrously wrong paths.

Soon after his return from Carpi, Machiavelli published yet another work in his rapidly expanding *oeuvre*. This was a treatise titled *The Art of War*, which was completed the previous autumn and, on August 16, 1521, came off the press of Filippo di Giunta, a celebrated Florentine printer who specialized in Greek texts. Another product of his discussions in the Orti Oricellari, it was dedicated to Lorenzo Strozzi, the thirty-nine-year-old son-in-law of the late Bernardo Rucellai, author of the comedies *Pisana* and *Falargo*, and (more important) the man who had introduced Machiavelli to the Archbishop of Florence. In the dedication Machiavelli explains that he is writing what he has learned about the art of war because he still believes it possible "to bring military practice back to ancient methods and to restore some forms of earlier excellence."

Set in the Orti Oricellari in the year 1516, *The Art of War* takes the form of a dialogue and may have been loosely based on actual conversations. One of the main characters is the mercenary Fabrizio Colonna, who had died in March 1520 and could not therefore have disputed the arguments (such as, ironically, an attack on the use of mercenaries) that Machiavelli put into his mouth. The work begins with Fabrizio stopping for a visit in Florence while en route from Lombardy to his domains near Naples. After enjoying entertainment in the Palazzo Rucellai, he wanders with Cosimo Rucellai and the other guests among the groves of the Orti Oricellari, where he spots various odd-looking plants. Cosimo informs him that, however rare they might seem, these plants were actually common in the gardens of the ancient Romans, and that his grandfather Bernardo, founder of the gardens, revived their ancient methods of cultivation. Fabrizio tut-tuts this kind of veneration of the past, deploring the fact that, among all the glories of ancient Rome, such inconsequential pursuits, ones that lead to indolence and decadence, should have been the ones adopted by modern-day Italians. Fabrizio—and by extension Machiavelli—would much rather see the ancient Roman warrior spirit rekindling itself in Italian breasts.

Discussion therefore turns to military matters, with Fabrizio becoming Machiavelli's spokeman for how a military force should be organized and battles fought. Like so many of his works, it is drenched in nostalgia for the power and glory of Republican Rome. Unsurprisingly, there is a plea for a citizen militia, an obsession that not even the disaster of Prato could dislodge from Machiavelli's brain. Other hobbyhorses also appear. The treatise is intended as a practical handbook for military organization, with Fabrizio stressing, for example, that army encampments should be exactly 1,360 feet long and their tents 30 feet deep and 60 feet wide. This apparently hands-on precision cannot disguise the fact that many of the book's prescriptions would have been quite disastrous in sixteenth-century warfare. Most seriously, Machiavelli downgrades the importance of artillery, having Fabrizio declare, ludicrously, that any advantages of heavy ordnance are offset by its blinding clouds of smoke. This is a repetition of the argument made a few years earlier in the *Discourses*, where Machiavelli's exhortations for his fellow Italians to emulate the ancient Romans made him reluctant to endorse both artillery and cavalry for the simple reason that the ancient Romans had used them either sparingly or not at all. He offers as an example of the supremacy of the infantry a campaign waged by Crassus against the Parthians in 53 B.C.—as if methods of ancient warfare were still applicable in the days of gunpowder.

This oversight is perverse given that recent history had shown Machiavelli the dreadful power of cannons and firearms. It is to his discredit that he so drastically underrates artillery at a time when Alfonso d'Este was transforming the state of warfare with cannon fire, unleashed to such devastating effect at Ravenna. Even more recently, a French victory over the Swiss at Marignano in 1515 had displayed the vast superiority of the artillery over the infantry: the fabled Swiss pikemen had simply been no match for French cannons. No citations from ancient authors could overturn that stark and inarguable truth.

This presumption that ancient Roman methods of warfare

were still applicable in the first decades of the sixteenth century highlights a persistent problem in Machiavelli's thinking. He is guilty of making an *argumentum ad antiquitam*, whereby the authority and expertise of the Romans is too readily accepted and too widely applied. Francesco Guicciardini was no doubt referring to his friend when he observed: "Those who quote the Romans on everything are greatly deceiving themselves. They mistakenly suppose that our state exists under exactly the same conditions and can be governed on exactly the same model."[1] Machiavelli claimed in the prologue to the *Discourses* that it was possible for his countrymen to imitate the ancient Romans because human nature remained unchanged. Yet some things were more readily imitated than others. In fact, in the previous century, Italian culture had been rebuilding and renewing itself with reference to the examples of antiquity. But it was one thing for an architect like Leon Battista Alberti to build a church or a palazzo according to Roman models, or for Ariosto to write comedies based on the plays of Plautus or Terence— quite another for generals to conduct themselves with fidelity to 1,500-year-old models. The art of warfare and slaughter had been greatly improved since the days of Crassus.

Machiavelli's meditations on warfare, however potentially misguided, were grimly opportune. Within a fortnight of *The Art of War* coming off the press, the papal and imperial armies were once again fighting the French. In May, while Machiavelli was in Carpi, Leo X had concluded a secret treaty with Charles V, the twenty-one-year-old grandson of Maximilian, with the aim of ousting the French from Milan, retaken by King François I after the decisive Battle of Marignano. By 1521, Leo was actually less interested in driving the "barbarians" from Italy than in safeguarding the possessions of both the Holy See and the Medici family should war break out, as seemed inevitable, between François and Charles. Leo had originally tried to forge an alliance against the Holy Roman Emperor with the assistance of France, England, and Venice; but after negotiations proceeded slowly he was won over in the spring of 1521 by the blandishments of Charles, who offered him Piacenza, Parma, and Ferrara as well as imperial protection for Florence.

Hostilities began in August, with the combined armies of Leo and Charles, commanded by Fabrizio Colonna's cousin, Prospero, dislodging the French from some of their Italian possessions. A few months later, in November, Milan was seized and most of Lombardy occupied. Leo did not live to savor his victory, since he died on the first of December, ten days before his forty-sixth birthday, following a reign of almost nine years. He apparently succumbed to malaria, though naturally there were rumors of poison.

The death of Leo X had obvious ramifications for his cousin's rule in Florence. The archbishop was a wiser and more moderate leader than either Giuliano or Lorenzo di Piero had been, but his skill and courtesy could not disguise the fact that the government of Florence was still run from the Palazzo Medici, not the Palazzo della Signoria. Without the guarantee of papal protection, he and his family were vulnerable for the first time in almost a decade. His enemies, sensing the opportunity, started mobilizing early in 1522. The leader was Piero Soderini's brother, Cardinal Francesco, the Bishop of Volterra and for many years a close friend of Machiavelli. With the money and blessing of the King of France, Cardinal Soderini hired a *condottiere* named Renzo da Ceri and began advancing north from Siena with the express purpose of unseating the archbishop and reestablishing a more broadly based republic. The campaign was quickly crushed, however, thanks to a pro-Medici force led by another *condottiere*, Orazio Baglioni, the twenty-nine-year-old illegitimate son of Gianpaolo Baglioni of Perugia.

A further blow was then struck against Cardinal Soderini's hopes for his family's restoration when early in June a plot against the life of the archbishop was uncovered in Florence. The assassination attempt was to have been carried out on June 19, the Feast of Corpus Christi, by two men even closer to Machiavelli than Cardinal Soderini: Zanobi Buondelmonti and Luigi Alamanni, the men to whom he had dedicated his *Life of Castruccio Castracani*. Their coconspirators included several of Machiavelli's other "noontime friends" from the Orti Oricellari. Zanobi and Luigi managed to escape, but two of their accomplices were apprehended and speedily beheaded, while Cardinal Soderini was imprisoned in Rome on orders of the new pope, Adrian VI. The final act in this tragedy was the death in Rome on June 13, following ten years of exile, of the man around whom the hopes for a new republic had swirled, Piero Soderini.

This failed plot and its aftermath were a terrible personal disaster for Machiavelli. Not only was the literary group in the gardens of the Palazzo Rucellai disbanded, but a number of his closest friends were either dead or in exile. As in the case of the plot against the Medici in 1513, questions surround whether or not Machiavelli was involved in, or knew about, the planned assassination. His close association with Zanobi Buondelmonti and the other ringleaders, together with his troubled relationship with the Medici, certainly raises clouds of suspicion. However, his biographers have unanimously acquitted him of any direct involvement, as did the authorities in 1522. Buondelmonti had supposedly discussed with his coconspirators the possibility of including Machiavelli in the plot but was advised that his friend's reputation as a Medici opponent could compromise their plans.

Even if Machiavelli was not involved in the conspiracy, questions also arise as to whether or not he might have approved of it. Certainly he would have been a beneficiary of a new regime instituted by Cardinal Soderini, and he would have been more in sympathy with its constitution than with the rule of the archbishop. But what were his thoughts on such conspiracies in general? Would it have been justifiable, in his opinion, to murder the Archbishop of Florence in order to establish a more popular regime?

Machiavelli's finest biographer, Roberto Ridolfi, contends that Machiavelli regarded political assassination as "a grave crime."[2] Yet the evidence of Machiavelli's writings offers a more ambiguous testimony. Numerous references to assassinations and conspiracies are found in the *Discourses*, which was dedicated to Zanobi Buondelmonti. The second chapter of the book discusses, with approval, a hypothetical conspiracy in which a republican government is founded after leading citizens rise up to overthrow a corrupt leader. Such conspiracies are carried out, he writes, "by those who in nobility, greatness of spirit, riches, and rank were superior to the others, such as could not endure the shameful life of their prince." Sanction is clearly given for men with nobility and greatness of spirit to overthrow a corrupt or tyrannical leader.

A more extended treatment of the question is given in the chapter of the *Discourses* entitled "Of Conspiracies." This chapter is, at almost 9,000 words, by far the longest in the entire book—an indication that in 1517 Machiavelli and friends like Buondelmonti were debating the issue in earnest. The chapter functions as a kind of conspirator's handbook. Full of helpful suggestions for would-be conspirators, it describes various political conspiracies and analyzes how and why they failed. Machiavelli stipulates, for example, that a conspirator's plans ought never to be communicated to anyone else except under the most urgent necessity, and even then only to persons who are to be trusted absolutely. He also specifies—perhaps remembering the piece of paper with its list of names so carelessly dropped by Agostino Capponi—that nothing should ever be put in writing. A more chilling prescription is that no one should be left alive who will be able to take revenge. He cites as a cautionary tale the killers of Girolamo Riario, who unwisely left Caterina Sforza alive to wreak her bloody vengeance. He also discusses the relative merits of using the sword versus using poison (dismissing the latter as unreliable).

Equally revealing are Machiavelli's observations on political assassination in his history of Florence, the work he was composing at the time of the 1522 conspiracy. This book includes a description of the murder of Caterina Sforza's father, Galeazzo Maria, knifed by assassins in Milan in 1476. He recounts how the young conspirators wished to rid Milan of the cruel and licentious duke and establish a popular government. The ardently republican spirit of the ringleader, Cola Montano, was, in Machiavelli's eyes, an extremely noble and worthy one that easily justified the murder of a tyrant like Galeazzo Maria Sforza. Machiavelli laments the deaths of the assassins, and into the mouth of one of them, twenty-three-year-old Girolamo Olgiato, executed for his part in the plot, he puts some heroic last words: *"Mors acerba, fama perpetua, stabit vetus memoria facti"* ("Death is bitter, fame everlasting; long will the memory of my deed endure").

These words were composed not long after the failed conspiracy against the archbishop. It is not difficult to read in Machiavelli's wistful regret for "these unhappy young men" his sorrow for his friends from the Orti Oricellari. Machiavelli certainly mourned the deaths of his friends and the exile of Buondelmonti and Alamanni, but he would not necessarily have deplored their conspiracy or denounced it as a crime.

Chapter Nineteen

FLORENCE HELD FEW charms for Machiavelli after the breakup of the literary group in the Orti Oricellari. He seems to have spent most of the following two years in the country at Sant' Andrea in Percussina, writing his history and tending to the business of his farm. He was still snaring thrushes (his brother-in-law received a gift of thirty birds at the end of 1522) and supervising the harvest and sale of his crops. He was also dealing with the affairs of his brother, Totto, who had died in June 1522, adding yet more sorrow and loss to what had been a desolate month.

Another concern for Machiavelli was the conduct of his second son, Lodovico, a wayward and difficult young man. Early in 1523 he wrote to his old friend Francesco Vettori bemoaning the fate of fathers cursed with sons. Among other things, he was worried about nineteen-year-old Lodovico's relationship with another young man: "He plays with him, sports with him, walks about with him, whispers in his ear; they sleep in the same bed." The metamorphosis of Machiavelli the bawdy voluptuary into a prim, disapproving moralist must have taken Vettori by surprise. Having sown several hectares of wild oats himself, Vettori took a more broad-minded view of Lodovico's conduct, reminding Machiavelli that "as we grow old, we become too morose and, so to speak, finicky, and we do not remember what we did when we were young."

It is a superb irony that the author of *La Mandragola* should suddenly appear in the role of the crusty old patriarch, at odds with his adolescent son. Still, Machiavelli's anxieties about Lodovico's sexual conduct are surprising given his own emancipated behavior. He seems to have taken—at least when Lodovico was not implicated—a lenient attitude toward what was known across Europe as the "Florentine vice." One of his closest friends in Florence, a shopkeeper named Donato del Corno, was homosexual. His shop—which Machiavelli frequented so much that Donato called him a "shop pest"—seems to have been something of a haunt for other homosexuals. Whether Machiavelli himself ever actually took male lovers is uncertain, though at one point in his career he became the subject of bizarre gossip. In 1500, Ottaviano Ripa, a member of the Ten of Liberty and Peace, stopped by the Chancellery and, in the course of conversation with Agostino Vespucci and several other secretaries, speculated that Machiavelli might encounter "grave danger" during his stay in France "since sodomites and homosexuals are stringently prosecuted there." When Vespucci objected that Machiavelli's character was "excellent and spotless," Ripa responded with an absurd tale about Machiavelli having been sodomized by a horse—a rumor that surely reveals more about Ripa's leisurely timetable and his gullible (or malicious) disposition than it does about Machiavelli's erotic adventures.

Machiavelli was not so morose and finicky that he could no longer find himself ensnared in Venus's "nets of gold." His affair with the abandoned wife of Niccolò Tafani—if in fact it ever amounted to much—seems to have been far in the past; but early in 1524 he began another love affair, this time with a singer named Barbera Raffacani. He met her at the home of Jacopo Falconetti, a brickmaker and lime-burner known as Il Fornaciaio (from *fornace*, "furnace"). Lime-burning was a noxious process detrimental to the health of anyone living downwind. Falconetti made huge profits from his business— which provided the construction industry with ingredients for lime-mortar—and bought himself a comfortable villa and gardens a short distance southwest of Florence, at Santa Maria in Verzaia. At some point Falconetti had served on the Signoria before some unknown transgression saw him cashiered from office and banned from Florence for five years. Here, ensconced safely outside the Porta San Frediano, he made the most of his exile by entertaining groups of friends in sumptuous style.

Machiavelli was invited to join these gatherings in 1524. His seat at the table was earned thanks to *La Mandragola* rather than *The Prince* or the *Discourses*. Falconetti's banquets entirely lacked the highbrow political debate of the Orti Oricellari; but Machiavelli, the epicurean who could eat enough for "six dogs and three wolves," would have enjoyed them no less for that. In fact, food had probably been what brought Machiavelli and Falconetti together in the first place. They seem to have met at an eccentric Florentine dining club called the Compagnia della Cazzuola (the "Fellowship of the Trowel").* The pleasure-loving members of this group had been coming together since about 1512 for gorgeous feasts in which guests vied with one another to create the most inventive and beautiful fare. One member, the painter Andrea del Sarto, once presented a truly memorable dish. He offered the company an eight-sided temple made from marzipan, with sausages for columns, pastry cornices, and colored mosaics made out of jelly. Inside was a pulpit carved from cold veal, a Bible of macaroni paste with peppercorn writing, and a choir made up of thrushes dressed in surplices and arranged with their beaks open as if in song. Two fat pigeons took the bass parts, while six larks served as sopranos.[1] Machiavelli may have supplied the thrushes for this edible choir, since Andrea supplied the painted scenery for a performance of *La Mandragola* staged for the Compagnia della Cazzuola sometime in 1523. Falconetti was either at this performance—which took place ten miles outside Florence, at Monteloro—or else he learned of it soon afterward. At the

---

* This group took its name from a comic incident at a dinner hosted in the garden of a hunchbacked musician by the name of Feo d'Agnolo. One of the guests, spotting a trowel left by a workman, charged it with mortar and then popped it into Feo's mouth as he opened wide for some ricotta cheese. The trowel thereafter became their symbol.

beginning of 1524 he was planning a performance at his own home to celebrate the end of his banishment. Machiavelli offered to write a new play for him instead—one in which he would give a role to Barbera Raffacani.

Barbera, who used the *nom de guerre* Barbera Fiorentina, was undoubtedly a courtesan. Machiavelli's friend Francesco Guicciardini called her as much, dismissing her in a teasing letter as "meretricious company" and claiming that she "strives, as does her kind, to please everyone." She was much younger than Machiavelli, and the discrepancy between their ages partly inspired the plot of the play he wrote for Falconetti's entertainment. Entitled *Clizia*, it involves an old man named Nicomaco—an obvious play on Machiavelli's own name— who competes with his son, Cleandro, for the love of a young woman named Clizia. The play's depiction of the follies of an old man pursuing a younger woman suggests that Machiavelli had certainly not lost his sense of humor, as does the picture of a father-son falling-out in which there may be shades of Machiavelli's own tension with his son Lodovico.

Machiavelli worked on the five-act play—somewhat hastily, judging by the end product—in the latter half of 1524, completing it on time for a performance at the start of 1525. He was actually translating and adapting as much as he was composing, since most of the plot comes from a farce called *Casina* written by Plautus and first staged in about 185 B.C. Machiavelli transplanted the action to Florence during the Carnival of 1506. The play begins on the day that Nicomaco—described unflatteringly as a "crazy, drooling, blear-eyed, toothless old man"—

has chosen for the wedding of his beautiful young ward, the orphan girl Clizia, who has lived in his household for the past dozen years. Refusing to allow his love-struck son, Cleandro, to wed Clizia, he plans to marry her instead to his obliging servant, Pirro, who will allow Nicomaco to sleep with her whenever he pleases. Nicomaco's wife, Sofronia, understandably, has other ideas. She foils him by dressing a male servant in Clizia's clothes and slyly substituting him into the marriage bed. Nicomaco eagerly tiptoes into the bedroom after having dosed himself with a powerful aphrodisiac "that would rejuvenate a man of ninety." After a tussle under the covers, he is alarmed to feel a "hard, pointed object" in the bed. The servant then throws back the cover and makes a rude gesture at the stunned Nicomaco. "I am disgraced for all eternity," the old man laments as the remainder of the cast convulses with laughter at his folly and misfortune.

The play features many of the same ingredients as *La Mandragola*, including witty wordplay, topical references, a foolish and risible old man who is cleverly duped, and what modern-day censors might call content of a sexual nature. On the whole, though, it is not as successful as *La Mandragola*, mostly because Machiavelli chooses to describe action—such as the bedroom encounter between Nicomaco and the servant—rather than to show it onstage. The results are several long speeches of exposition rather than the fast-paced farce of the earlier play. In *La Mandragola*, for example, we see the urine sample flourished onstage, whereas in *Clizia* we hear about—but never see—the aphrodisiac that is powerful enough to "wake up a regiment." For dramatic purposes, the difference is immense.

That much said, the play was a huge success when it was staged at Falconetti's villa on January 13, 1525. Machiavelli's reputation as a dramatist "aroused in everyone the desire to see it." Falconetti sent out invitations not only to the patricians of Florence but also to the middle-class merchants and even (quite exceptionally) to the poorer people. Huge crowds—some elements of which were boisterously behaved—poured through the Porta San Frediano for the short trip to Santa Maria in Verzaia. No expense was spared to make the evening a success. Part of Falconetti's garden had been leveled to make a stage, and the set was designed by the painter Bastiano da Sangallo, the nephew of Machiavelli's friend Giuliano da Sangallo and one of Michelangelo's assistants in the Sistine Chapel. Nymphs and shepherds frolicked onstage during the opening song, "Blessed Is This Happy Day," which had been composed by Machiavelli and sung—like those between the acts—by Barbera. The play's success won Machiavelli a huge celebrity. "The fame of your comedy has flown all over," a friend wrote to him a short while later from Modena. "You and Fornaciaio have managed things so that the fame of your revelries has spread and continues to spread not only throughout all Tuscany but also throughout Lombardy." The Wheel of Fortune was spinning on a very curious axis: the man who had won fame with his militia in 1509, only to be disgraced in 1512, had now won glory as a writer of ribald comedies.

Machiavelli still nourished hopes for another sort of glory.

Within a few weeks of the triumphant performance of *Clizia*, he had completed his history of Florence. Four years in the making, the work was a hefty 170,000-word pagemonster and covered a thousand years of Florentine history, from the barbarian invasions to the death of Lorenzo the Magnificent. The manuscript was now ready to be presented to the man who had commissioned it. For that, Machiavelli would need to travel to Rome.

Pope Adrian VI, a Dutchman, had died in September 1523, only twenty months into his reign. In the conclave that followed, Giulio de' Medici, the Archbishop of Florence, was elected Pope Clement VII. Once again a Medici wore the papal tiara, and once again it seemed Florence would profit from an alliance with the Church.

The accession of Clement VII had obvious consequences for Florentine politics. Clement was elected thanks in part to the endorsement of the Holy Roman Emperor, Charles V, whom he had supported in the days when he controlled papal policy under Leo X. His election coincided with the movement into Lombardy of a 27,000-strong French invasion force with which François I hoped to recapture Milan from Prospero Colonna and the imperial troops. Hesitant and equivocal by nature, Clement began pursuing the kind of weather-cock politics—the vacillating *via di mezzo*—that had so infuriated Machiavelli when it was pursued by the Florentine Signoria. Anxiously gauging the relative strengths of the French and imperial forces, the pope began detaching himself from his former ally, the emperor, and dealing secretly with the King of France. The French recapture of Milan in November 1524 prompted him into a commitment, and a month later he signed a secret treaty with François against the emperor.

The alliance proved, from the outset, a terrible disaster. Within two months, on February 23, 1525, French forces were crushed by the emperor's army on the field of battle at Pavia. Twelve thousand French soldiers were either killed or wounded and the great French commander Louis de la Trémoïlle was slain. François himself was taken prisoner—the first reigning monarch to be taken in battle since King John II of France was captured by the English at Poitiers in 1356. Milan was promptly reconquered by the imperial forces, leaving Clement at the mercy of the emperor.

This was the infelicitous moment at which Machiavelli proposed to travel to Rome and present the pope with his *History of Florence*. He was warned by a friend, however, that "the times are opposed to reading and to gifts," and so in the end he did not travel south until May, when a treaty was signed between Charles V and the Church. Clement, who said he believed the work would "give pleasure," duly accepted the history and paid Machiavelli 120 florins—twenty florins more than the agreed amount—out of his own purse.

The pope might not have been quite so generous with his money had he actually read the book first. Most previous histories of Florence were extended hymns of praise to the city; their premise was usually the patriotic one taken by Leonardo Bruni, whose *Laudatio Florentinae urbis*, composed in 1403, gushed that "Florence is of such a nature that a more distinguished or more splendid city cannot be found on the entire earth." The pages of Machiavelli's chronicle, on the other hand, tell a bleak and unrelenting story of factionalism, violence, rampant corruption, political incompetence, eroded liberties, and almost comically inept military skirmishes led by unscrupulous *condottieri*. There is even a grisly description of an episode of cannibalism that took place in Florence in 1343, as well as a horrific account of the Pazzi Conspiracy of 1478—the political assassination in which Clement VII's father, Giuliano de' Medici, the brother of Lorenzo the Magnificent, lost his life.

His portrayal of the Medici gave Machiavelli great anxiety as he composed the work. How was he to tell the history of this family whose members had overthrown Florence's republican constitution and, in his opinion, trampled the city's liberties? His dedication to Clement VII at the start of the book warns that he may seem grudging in his praise of the Medici, but he claims to have been instructed by the pope himself to write the history of his ancestors in a way free of flattery and excess adulation. He is not, it must be said, entirely skimping in his praise. He makes Cosimo de' Medici sound like a hero from *The Prince* as he describes how Cosimo's prudence, wealth, and "way of living" made him "feared and loved" by the people of Florence. But he offers numerous criticisms of the family, including a particularly pointed one in his account of the Pazzi Conspiracy. In what amounts to a kind of *apologia* for the assassins, he claims the attempt on the life of Lorenzo took place because the Medici were trying to gain absolute authority in the city. With blithe disregard for the fact that his patron's father died in the attack, he recounts how "the government was so completely limited to the Medici, who had seized such great authority, that the discontented were forced either with patience to bear that kind of government or, if they did attempt to destroy it, to do so with conspiracies and secretly." These conspirators were not dissimilar, in Machiavelli's view, from those who cut down Galeazzo Maria Sforza a few years earlier.

Yet all is not completely lost in this gloomy survey of Florentine history. The book strikes a familiar note, with Machiavelli remarking in his preface how, had the city ever managed to unite itself, its people would have surpassed all other republics, both ancient and modern. His reason for this optimism is the power of the arms and industry possessed by the city, and in particular the citizen militia of 1,200 cavalry and 12,000 infantry that, in former days, the republic was able to muster from among its own citizens.

A citizen militia was not, of course, a matter simply of nostalgia for Machiavelli. He took the opportunity while presenting his manuscript to bend the pope's ear about establishing militias throughout the Papal States in order to defend the interests of the Holy See. Anxious to protect himself against the influence and encroachments of the emperor, Clement paid close attention and then ordered Machiavelli to Faenza, in the Romagna, to investigate the feasibility of such a project. Machiavelli left Rome with a papal brief stating that he was to engage himself in "a matter of great importance" on which depends "the safety of the Papal States as well as that of the whole of Italy, and practically the whole of Christendom." Hyperbole to be sure. The brief says more about Machiavelli's powers of persuasion than it does about the necessity or efficacy of any projected militia. However, one aspect of the brief was accurate: Italy and the whole of Christendom were indeed plunging into the gravest danger.

Musters and parades in the chill air, drums beating and boots marching, pike squares shaping themselves in the piazza, banners flying and bells ringing. As he rode back north in June, Machiavelli must have been dreaming about a return to the work he had done in the rugged villages of the Casentino more than a dozen years earlier. The fact that his fifty-sixth birthday had passed a few weeks before he traveled to Rome does not seem to have blunted his energy or eagerness, and he rode on to Faenza almost immediately. There he joined forces with Francesco Guicciardini, recently appointed governor of the Romagna. Alas, Guicciardini quickly doused the militia plan with cold water. He pointed out, among other things, that a papal militia would need to be founded on a love of the Church—a quality distinctly lacking in the tough peasants of the Romagna. The plan was ultimately rejected by the pope, and Machiavelli was back in Florence before the end of July.

The trip to Faenza was not without its rewards, since Machiavelli had made the acquaintance there of a courtesan named Maliscotta. She was said to have been charmed by his "manners and conversation." Furthermore, he and Guicciardini began planning a performance of *La Mandragola* in Faenza. This project gave him the excuse, once he was back in Florence, to continue keeping company with Barbera Fiorentina. "I have been dining these last few evenings with Barbera and discussing the play," he wrote at the end of September. He composed a number of songs for her to sing between the acts, including one entitled "How Gentle Is Deception"—a cheerful celebration of the kind of deceit that he had praised a dozen years earlier in *The Prince*.

The work was to be staged in early 1526, but at the last minute it was canceled. Guicciardini had been summoned urgently to Rome by the pope to discuss momentous political developments. Shortly afterward, in March 1526, Machiavelli, too, was summoned to Rome. Florence was threatened with invasion and—as in the old days—looked to Machiavelli for its salvation.

Chapter Twenty

ONCE AGAIN, A war appeared inevitable. It began, like so many others, with a peace treaty. On January 14, 1526, the King of France and the Emperor Charles V signed the Treaty of Madrid, under whose terms François surrendered all claims on Italian territories, including Milan, Naples, and Genoa. He was then released from his captivity—he had been held since the Battle of Pavia—but his two young sons were taken as hostages to ensure his compliance with the terms of the treaty. It soon became obvious that François had no plans whatsoever to comply.

The supremacy of the emperor in Italy and the complete destruction of French fortunes were of the utmost concern to the pope. If Julius II had formed his Holy League in 1511 with the aim of driving the French from Italy, the imperial dominance was what led Clement VII to inaugurate a new Holy League. This compact, signed in Cognac on May 22, 1526, created a powerful alliance against the emperor; its signatories were France, the papacy, Florence, and Venice. The participation of François broke the terms of the Treaty of Madrid, but Clement was happy to absolve him of the sin.

The urgency of the situation and its implications for Florence led to a swift resuscitation of Machiavelli's political fortunes. *The Art of War* had earned him such a reputation as a military engineer (its final section included a lengthy discussion of fortifications) that in the spring he was invited to Rome by Clement in order to discuss the state of Florence's defenses. He composed a report and was then promptly named Secretary and Quartermaster of the newly formed Curators of the Walls. His eldest son, Bernardo, twenty-two years old, would serve as his assistant. Father and son took with relish to the task of inspecting Florence's various fortifications. "My head is so full of ramparts that nothing else can enter it," Machiavelli informed Guicciardini in May. A month later, though, he had other things to think about as he was ordered to leave his ramparts and travel north to Lombardy, where fighting had already erupted, and where he was given the task of reorganizing an infantry to fight the enemy. The men were commanded by the *condottiere* Vitello Vitelli, the nephew, ironically, of Paolo and Vitellozzo Vitelli. Machiavelli found the men in such a "poor state" that he doubted they would do him much credit.

Arriving in Lombardy, at Marignano, ten miles southeast of Milan, Machiavelli must have felt his career had come full circle as he met the *capitano* of the Holy League's infantry. Giovanni de' Medici, better known as Giovanni delle Bande

Nere, was the twenty-eight-year-old son of Caterina Sforza, the woman with whom, in another age, Machiavelli had begun his political career. Giovanni was the great-grandson of Cosimo de' Medici's brother, Lorenzo and, as such, a distant relative of the pope; but in spirit he was more truly a Sforza, that race of valiant and brutal warriors. Then the most revered soldier in Europe, for the previous decade he had been the leader of an elite mercenary company called the Bande Nere, or "Black Bands," so named because they wore black armor and, since the death of Leo X, bordered their standards in black. Giovanni's military skill and daring were legendary, as were the Bande Nere's professionalism and devotion to their leader. The writer Pietro Aretino, famous for his character assassinations, had nothing but praise for Giovanni: "He was a born leader who had the art of making his men love and fear him. . . . Many might have envied him, but none could equal him."

Here, truly, was a man for Machiavelli to admire—a leader who seemed to have strode from the pages of *The Prince*, a man whom some had even begun celebrating with the name Giovanni d'Italia. And, indeed, Machiavelli duly sat up and took notice of this formidable soldier, whose personal emblem was, fittingly, a lightning bolt. Everyone agrees, he wrote to Guicciardini, that Giovanni delle Bande Nere "is brave and impetuous, has great ideas, and is a taker of bold decisions." Giovanni for his part was less impressed with Machiavelli. He seems to have read *The Art of War* and, doubting the wisdom of Machiavelli's various pronouncements, challenged him to drill 3,000 Bande Nere in the manner described in the book.

Machiavelli, unwisely, accepted the challenge, whereupon the parade ground at Marignano witnessed two hours of chaos. Giovanni finally put Machiavelli out of his misery, stepping forward to rally his troops with effortless aplomb. Afterward Giovanni claimed that "between him and Niccolò Machiavelli there was this difference: Niccolò knew how to write things well and he knew how to do them." If Machiavelli was unable to put the most skilled and disciplined troops in Europe through their paces, one begins to understand why the peasants from the Casentino failed so miserably at Prato.

Machiavelli redeemed himself somewhat in the weeks that followed, arranging for the surrender of Cremona to the forces of the Holy League. He then returned in early November to Florence, though not before stopping to consult a fortune-teller in Modena. This seer predicted disaster for the pope and the Holy League, claiming, as Machiavelli reported to Guicciardini, that "all the bad times were not over yet—both we and the pope will suffer greatly during them."

It did not take a prophet to foresee that catastrophe beckoned. With their ranks swelled by conscripts from Germany, many Lutherans among them, the imperial troops began their full-scale descent into Italy in November. They were led by Georg von Frundsberg, the Prince of Mindelheim, a veteran commander who wore around his neck a silk rope with which he had vowed to strangle the pope. Frundsberg's soldiers called themselves Landsknechts, or "men of the land." Pikemen trained in the tactics of the Swiss infantry, they wore flamboyant costumes—plumed hats, multicolored hose, bright doublets with slash-and-puff sleeves—that belied their dreadful efficiency.

The Landknechts landed a deadly blow early in the campaign. On November 25 they were engaged by the Bande Nere at Borgoforte, near Mantua. They had virtually no artillery except for four falconets—small swivel-mounted cannons that fired one-pound projectiles—supplied by Alfonso d'Este. They were bested in a skirmish by the swift, lightly armored Bande Nere, but one of the falconets found Giovanni, smashing his leg. The leg was amputated, but the great Medici warrior died five days later. His death was an incomparable loss for the Holy League.

Ferocious tacticians they might have been, but the thousands of imperial soldiers that crossed the Po in late November also bore a terrible resemblance to the army of Ramón de Cardona that had threatened Florence and sacked Prato in the summer of 1512. They were poorly provisioned, badly equipped, and many had not seen wages for several months. They had crossed the Alps via difficult and dangerous passes above Lake Garda, suffering (as Frundsberg noted) "poverty, hunger, and frost." As a result they were ill-disciplined and dangerous, bent on plundering Italian cities and—for the Lutherans in their ranks—chastising the corrupt papacy. The pope reasoned that such a force could be defeated with gold more easily than steel. At the end of January 1527 he signed a treaty with the emperor, promising to pay the starving soldiers 200,000 ducats if they marched back across the Alps. The situation might have been salvaged there and then had not a small and insignificant victory on the same day caused Clement to immediately repudiate the treaty and declare his antipathy for Charles. For the second time in little more than a year he had broken faith with the emperor. Joined a few days later by Spanish infantry under the command of the Duke of Bourbon, the imperial army, now 22,000-strong, began marching south toward Bologna. The Bande Nere, intact despite the loss of their leader, were ordered south to defend Rome.

With its enemy poised and its allies uncertain, the Republic of Florence was faced with its most dangerous crisis in fifteen years. In the first week of February, Machiavelli was sent to Parma to advise Francesco Guicciardini that Florence's situation looked desperate, with the city vulnerable to assault because of a lack of both money and soldiers. He was to find out from Guicciardini what military assistance Florence might expect from the pope and other allies such as the Venetians. To Machiavelli, though, matters did not appear entirely hopeless. Arriving in Parma on February 7, he began writing reports back to Florence insisting that Frundsberg's short supplies boded well for the Holy League. "It is believed that they are but little to be feared if they are not aided by our own disorders," he wrote of the imperial troops, "and all who have any experience in war judge that we ought to be victorious, unless either evil counsels or the lack of money cause our defeat." The lessons of 1512, clearly, had not been taken to heart.

From Parma, Machiavelli traveled through the snow to Bologna, where he kept an anxious eye on the activities of the imperial troops encamped a short distance away. He remained optimistic about Florence's chances of escaping or deflecting an attack. At the beginning of March he informed the Signoria that "no reasonable man" could suppose the soldiers would enter Tuscany due to the difficulty of the roads and the scarcity of supplies. "They would die of hunger in two days," he confidently predicted. Terrible rainstorms and blizzards also hampered the imperial troops—obstacles Machiavelli claimed had been "sent by the Almighty."

The efforts of the Almighty were soon undone, however, by his representative on earth. Clement's notorious shilly-shallying and double-dealing had inspired the poet Francesco Berni to satirize his papacy two years earlier as one of "yets and thens and buts and ifs and maybes, / Of many words that end in nothing." True to form, Clement changed his mind yet again. In the middle of March, as the enemy soldiers were storm-stayed on boggy ground ten miles outside Bologna, he tendered another truce. This time his offer—a miserly 60,000 ducats—caused outrage and mutiny in the imperial camp. Frundsberg had already suffered a stroke while trying in vain to control his unruly soldiers, and there seemed little chance that either their hunger or their savage hatred of the papacy could be allayed so cheaply. Machiavelli begged the Signoria to advance the money immediately to avert "the present evils and dangers," but within days it was clear to everyone but the pope—who foolishly dismissed the Bande Nere from Rome—that the truce was dead. Permanently incapacitated, Frundsberg was carried back to die on his German estates, while his ragged and half-starved troops clamored to move forward under the Duke of Bourbon. Virtually uncontrollable, they broke camp on March 31 and began marching in the direction of Florence, which, Machiavelli reported in alarm to the Signoria, "they regard as their prey."

Machiavelli had spent much time, the previous summer in Lombardy, fretting about Barbera Fiorentina. He wrote to Jacopo Falconetti for news of her and even urged powerful friends such as Francesco Guicciardini to look out for her interests, since "she gives me far more concern than does the emperor." In the spring of 1527, though, perhaps sensing the end was near, Machiavelli's thoughts turned to his family—to his wife, two daughters, and five sons, the youngest of whom, Totto, was a baby in the care of a wet nurse.

Machiavelli naturally worried about what might befall his family should the soldiers invade Tuscany. The farm at Sant' Andrea in Percussina, on the main road between Florence and Rome, was highly vulnerable. The family therefore moved into Florence and began arranging for the transport of their possessions, including twenty-three barrels of wine and olive oil, to a more secure location in the walled town of San Casciano. Even the beds were to be removed from the farm, denying any invaders the luxury of a comfortable night's sleep. If the imperial soldiers attacked Florence, Machiavelli reassured Marietta, he would immediately return to be with the family. "Christ watch over you all," he wrote.

Of all his children, Machiavelli seems to have been closest to his adolescent son Guido. On April 2 he wrote a long letter to the boy, urging him to do well in his studies ("take pains to learn letters and music") and promising to make him "a man of good standing if you are willing to do your share." He also offered a touching piece of advice about animal husbandry. One of the Machiavelli beasts at Sant' Andrea in Percussina, a young mule, had gone mad. Take the animal into the countryside, Machiavelli advised Guido, and remove the bridle and halter so the poor beast could "regain its own way of life and work off its craziness. The village is big and the beast is small." Guido soon reported back that the mule would be released into the meadow as soon as the grass was grown. He also proudly recounted how he was learning Latin participles and memorizing the first book of Ovid's *Metamorphoses*, which he hoped to recite to his father as soon as he returned. So often the truant husband and father, Machiavelli was suddenly anxious to see his family again. "I have never longed so much to return to Florence as I do now," he told Guido in a letter from Imola. He did not have long to wait, since he finally came home on April 22, after an absence of more than two months.

The threat from Bourbon's troops evaporated within days of Machiavelli's return. Florence was miraculously spared as the imperial army bypassed the city, judging the fortifications too difficult to breach without artillery. A greater and easier prize awaited Bourbon and his 22,000 rapacious soldiers. They began marching rapidly south, covering twenty miles per day, and on May 4 they had reached the walls of Rome. Bourbon demanded 300,000 ducats from the pope to turn around. The demand was refused and the assault on Rome began at dawn on Monday, May 6. Bourbon was killed outside the walls by a musketball (fired according to legend by the goldsmith Benvenuto Cellini) but his troops poured virtually unimpeded into the city. The pope fled into the Castel Sant' Angelo with several thousand other Romans; those remaining on the outside were robbed, ransomed, or raped as the invaders forced their way into palaces and convents in search of booty and women. The words of Luther may have been ringing in the ears of some of the Landsknechts, since he had denounced what he called "the whole brood of Roman Sodom," which he urged his followers to "attack with every sort of weapon and wash our hands in its blood."[1] Even so, the Catholic troops among the invaders behaved at least as abominably as the Germans. The Spaniards broke open and pillaged the tomb of Julius II, while the Italians—troops in the pay of Pompeo Colonna, an enemy of the pope—sacked and murdered at will. As many as 10,000 people died in the days that followed, and many treasures, both sacred and profane, went missing forever, including the golden cross of Constantine and the jeweled tiara of Nicholas V.

Machiavelli must have been appalled at the desolation as news of the terrible sack reached Florence on May 11. His description in *The Prince* of the lamentable state of Italy—"leaderless, lawless, crushed, despoiled, torn, overrun"—had never been more applicable. Now regarded as a faithful Medici servant, he was immediately sent to Civitavecchia, thirty-five miles northwest of Rome, where he was to help arrange the evacuation of the pope with Andrea Doria, admiral of the papal fleet. Clement may have been capable of rescue, but in Florence his rule was doomed. Within a week of the sack, on May 16, the Medici government—overseen since Clement's election by Silvio Passerini, the Cardinal of Cortona—collapsed. A more broadly based republic was quickly instituted, with both the Great Council of the People and the Ten of Liberty and Peace restored. Returning to Florence a few days afterward, Machiavelli was heard to sigh with regret "many times" when he learned how the city was free. His regret was not at the city's restored liberty, the return of the kind of popular government endorsed by him in works such as the *Discourses*. Rather, he despaired at his own dim prospects under a new regime. Desperate for so many years to take the Medici shilling, he suddenly had cause to bemoan this hard-won affiliation. Fortune had delivered yet another cruel blow.

Machiavelli's fears for his prospects proved well-founded. He hoped to return to his office in the Chancellery, but despite the intervention of his old friends Zanobi Buondelmonti and Luigi Alamanni, both back from exile, the post of Second Chancellor went to someone else. As in 1512, there would be no place for Machiavelli in the halls of power. This latest disappointment, following on from the shock of the furious attack on Rome, seems to have unsettled his ordinarily robust constitution. In the middle of June he fell ill with a stomach complaint and headaches. He treated the illness with pills—a mixture of aloe vera, saffron, and myrrh—that had seen him through previous physical crises. The medicine may have done more harm than good, because his condition quickly deteriorated. Friends such as Zanobi and Luigi as well as Filippo Strozzi hurried to his bedside.

Though desperately ill, "Machia" managed at some point to make his friends laugh with one final story. He told them of a dream in which he had seen a ragtag parade of poor, emaciated people. When he asked who they were, they replied that they were saints on their way to Paradise. On their heels came a contingent of men cutting a considerably different appearance, dressed as they were in courtly attire and solemnly discussing affairs of state. Among their ranks he spied philosophers and writers of antiquity such as Plato, Plutarch, and Tacitus. Asked where they were going, they explained that they were on their way to Hell. Machiavelli was in no doubt, as he quipped to his friends, whose company he would prefer. As Callimaco exclaims in *La Mandragola*: "How many excellent men have gone to Hell! Why should you be ashamed to go there too?"

This deathbed bravado notwithstanding, Machiavelli did take the usual precautions for the care of his soul. A priest, Brother Matteo, heard his sins and administered the last rites. According to his son Piero, then aged thirteen, Brother Matteo stayed with him to the end. The end came swiftly, and on the summer solstice, June 21, Machiavelli donned his robes and entered, it is to be hoped, the venerable courts of the ancients.

Conclusion

The Art of War was the only one of Machiavelli's works to be published in his lifetime. Though it circulated in manuscript, *The Prince* did not come off the printing press until more than four years after his death. In the summer of 1531, Pope Clement VII granted permission to Antonio Blado—the greatest printer in Rome during the sixteenth century—to publish the work, together with the *Discourses* and *The History of Florence*. Blado's edition appeared early in January 1532, by which time Clement had given sanction to Giunti, a Florentine printing firm, to prepare their own copies; the Florentine edition was then published in May of 1532. Works that had hitherto been accessible to only a select few now became available to a wider audience.

The Prince had earned Machiavelli a certain notoriety during his own lifetime. "Everyone hated him because of *The Prince*," one commentator observed around the time of Machiavelli's death. "The good thought him sinful, the wicked thought him more wicked or more capable than themselves, so that all hated him."[1] This was no doubt an exaggeration: Machiavelli was far better known as a popular dramatist and controversial state functionary than as the author of a tract on statecraft. Still, in the decades that followed, the hatred did indeed begin to curdle. Twenty-five years after its publication, Pope Paul IV placed *The Prince* in the severest category of the *Index librorum prohibitorum*, the Church's list of banned books; and by the end of the century Machiavelli had become, in some quarters, a near-mythical embodiment of evil, his name synonymous with hypocrisy and atheism. Elizabethan dramatists such as Christopher Marlowe and William Shakespeare used his name to create a diabolical stage villain. Marlowe's *The Jew of Malta*, first staged in 1591, begins with a prologue spoken by a character named "Machevill," who explains that he is presenting the tragedy of a Jew named Barabas who became wealthy through following Machiavelli's teachings. What follows is a display of ambition, avarice, treachery, and mass murder by the psychopathic Barabas, who ends up in a bubbling caudron of oil.

Since *The Prince* would not be translated into English until 1640, Marlowe and Shakespeare seem to have absorbed much of their devilish image of Machiavelli from Simon Patericke's 1577 translation of the *Contre-Machiavel*, a work by a French Protestant named Innocent Gentillet. Noting that the Queen of France, Catherine de' Medici, was the daughter of the man to whom *The Prince* had been dedicated, Gentillet blamed Machiavelli's doctrines for the St. Bartholomew's Day Massacre in August 1572, when thousands of French Protestants were murdered by Catholic mobs. The St. Bartholomew's Day Massacre was neither the first nor the last atrocity for which the blame was laid at Machiavelli's door. As early as 1539 an English cardinal, Reginald Pole, had condemned Machiavelli as "an enemy of the human race," arguing that Henry VIII's dissolution of the monasteries had been the upshot of his secret study of Machiavelli. Later it was claimed a Turkish translation of *The Prince* meant the Sultans had become more devoted than ever to strangling their brothers.

Whether or not Catherine de' Medici, Henry VIII, and the Turkish Sultans truly took their inspiration from *The Prince*, Machiavelli has suffered, more grievously than any other author, from guilt by association. Lorenzo di Piero de' Medici may have spurned the book in 1516, but few dictators or tyrants since then have neglected its lessons. Oliver Cromwell owned a manuscript copy; a well-thumbed edition accompanied Napoleon Bonaparte to the Battle of Waterloo; and Adolf Hitler admitted to keeping a copy on his bedside table. Small wonder that Henry Kissinger, in a 1972 interview with *The New Republic*, anxiously denied the influence on him of Machiavelli's doctrines. Others have been less reticent. Mafia bosses Carlo Gambino and John Gotti were both avowed students of Machiavelli, and the late Republican Party consultant Lee Atwater—notorious for his dirty-tricks campaigns in the 1980s—boasted he had read *The Prince* twenty-three times. When the late American rap artist Tupac Shakur desired a fearsome new epithet, he christened himself "Makaveli" in honor of the man whose works he studied during his eleven-month prison sentence in 1995.

Machiavelli's name has certainly become, in the popular imagination, a byword for treachery and mendacity. The *Oxford English Dictionary* defines a "machiavellian" as "an intriguer, an unscrupulous schemer." The term is even used by psychologists to describe a personality characterized by arrogance, dishonesty, cynicism, and manipulation.[2] Yet not everyone is agreed that these pejoratives truly characterize Machiavelli's thought. As long ago as the 1640s a French writer, Louis Machon, wrote *Apologie pour Machiavelle*, claiming the author of *The Prince* was really a misunderstood Christian moralist. A 1954 book by Giuseppe Prezzolini, satirically entitled *Machiavelli anticristo*, argued that religious and political prejudice, combined with sheer ignorance, have conspired to make him the most flagrantly misunderstood thinker in history; and fifty years later Machiavelli was still, according to the subtitle of a book by Michael White, "a man misunderstood."

In fact, Machiavelli has long enjoyed an eminent reputation drastically at odds with the one-dimensional image of the dishonest and manipulative stage villain. Immediately before the heyday of Marlowe and Shakespeare, in 1585, he was praised by the Italian jurist Alberico Gentili, later Regius Professor of Civil Law at the University of Oxford, as a man of prudence and wisdom who defended democracy and despised tyranny. For Denis Diderot and Jean-Jacques Rousseau (both of whom believed *The Prince* was intended as a satire),[3] Machiavelli was an advocate of republicanism and liberty, while Benedetto Croce and Leo Strauss have christened him the founder of the new "science" of politics. During the Risorgimento, Machiavelli was glorified as a patriot and advocate of Italian unification, a view more recently maintained (with added sophistication) by historians and political scientists such as Garrett Mattingly, Eric Vögelin, and Maurizio Viroli. Other political scientists have celebrated him as one of the foundational figures of modern Western thought whose legacy is not violence and treachery but theories of classical republicanism, political liberty, and civic virtue that influenced, among others, the framers of the American Constitution.[4]

Machiavelli is certainly a complex thinker whose writings belie the popular view of him as the messenger of a simple doctrine of conquest through iniquitous stratagems. Yet his intricacies have spawned a bewildering number of interpretations. A 1971 essay by Isaiah Berlin in the *New York Review of Books* recounted some twenty widely divergent readings of *The Prince*, from Bertrand Russell's description of it as a "handbook for gangsters" to a Bolshevik author's praise for the work's dialectical grasp of the realities of power that made it a forerunner of Marx and Lenin. "What other writer," asks Berlin, "has caused his readers to disagree about his purposes so deeply and so widely?" Further interpretations have been added since 1971, including an intriguing feminist reading that sees the work as a "family drama" anxiously pitting masculine enterprises such as law and politics against the dark and volatile feminine agency of Fortune.[5]

Machiavelli has not, therefore, been across-the-board demonized or unfairly misunderstood—among more discerning readers, at least—as a preacher of the straightforward message of evil. On the contrary: he has been conscripted into service by adherents of varying political outlooks eager to unfurl his banner over their causes. That Enlightenment thinkers such as Diderot and Rousseau should have found in Machiavelli a spokesman for political liberty; that nineteenth-century Italian patriots regarded him as an impassioned advocate of Italian unification; that Bolsheviks hailed him as a Marxist-Leninist outrider; that a late twentieth-century feminist academic found in his writings anxieties about the female threat to male power—these and other interpretations suggest that Machiavelli's thought is strangely malleable to any number of diametrically opposing ideologies and approaches. The sheer variety and sophistication of these appropriations pay testament to the variety and sophistication of his writings.

The diversity of these interpretations also pays testament to Machiavelli's numerous antinomies. His writings bulge with contradictions that the most astute political scientists still struggle to reconcile. Was Machiavelli really a theorist of iron-fisted despotism? Or was he a republican patriot who exalted liberty and popular government? Many of the statements in *The Prince* are undeniably at odds with those in the *Discourses*—works, furthermore, fraught with their own internal contradictions.

The key to some of these ambiguities may lie in the nature of the man himself. Machiavelli's numerous undertakings—diplomat, playwright, poet, historian, political theorist, farmer, military engineer, militia captain—make him, like his friend Leonardo, a true Renaissance man. Yet, like Leonardo, who denounced the "beastly madness" of war while devising ingenious and deadly weapons, Machiavelli is awash in paradoxes and inconsistencies. He was a strikingly modern thinker who paved the way for a science of politics, yet he also readily put his faith in astrologers and fortune-tellers. He was a lover of liberty who believed our freedom to act was severely curtailed by the law of necessity. He composed treatises advising leaders how to rule at the same time that he expected them always and inevitably to act according to their own ungovernable natures. He was a defender of republicanism who was willing to offer his services to the family that dismantled the Florentine republic and suppressed its liberties. He admired dissimulation (and even composed a poem in praise of deception) even though he himself was constitutionally unable to flatter or deceive.

Probably his greatest contradiction was that he understood better than anyone else in the sixteenth century how to seize and maintain political power—and yet, deprived of power himself in 1512, he spent many long years in the political wilderness, making a series of bungling and fruitless attempts to regain his position. The man who popularized the notion that Fortune could be beaten into submission offers a lamentable illustration of what he once called the goddess's "great and remitting malice."

This battle against Fortune was a constant both in Machiavelli's life and in his writings. "How my evil fortune grieves me," laments Cleandro in *Clizia*. "I seem born never to get what I want." These words might have served as Machiavelli's epitaph. As it is, his tomb features a different inscription. On June 22, 1527, he was buried alongside his father in the church of Santa Croce in Florence. Centuries later, in 1787, a grand new tomb in the south aisle was carved for him by Innocenzo Spinazzi. A few steps from the tombs of Michelangelo, Galileo, and Leonardo Bruni, the marble monument features an allegorical figure of Diplomacy above the proud legend TANTO NOMINI NVLLVM PAR ELOGIVM: "No elegy is equal to such a name." Fortune has not, at least in his posterity, treated Machiavelli quite so badly after all.

Acknowledgments

M Y THANKS ARE due to Professor William R. Cook, Dr. Mark Asquith, Larry Goldstone, Nancy Goldstone, and my agent, Christopher Sinclair-Stevenson, all of whom offered comments and advice on earlier versions of the text. Lauro Martines kindly answered several of my queries, and Gary N. Curtis offered advice on logical fallacies. For their many and various exertions on my behalf, I am likewise grateful to James Atlas, Jessica Fjeld, and Janet Min Lee. Most of all I must thank my wife, Melanie, who happily confutes Machiavelli's opinion of wedlock.

Notes

CHAPTER I

1. Francesco Guicciardini, *The History of Italy*, trans. Sidney Alexander (New York: Macmillan, 1969), p. 127. On "Brother Girolamo's caterpillars," see Luca Landucci, *A Florentine Diary from 1450 to 1516*, ed. Iodoco del Badia, trans. Alice de Rosen Jervis (London: J.M. Dent & Sons, 1927), pp. 144–45.

2. James B. Atkinson and David Sices, eds., *Machiavelli and His Friends: Their Personal Correspondence* (DeKalb, Illinois: Northern Illinois University Press, 1996), p. 222. All further quotations from Machiavelli's personal letters will be from this edition.

3. Catherine Atkinson, *Debts, Dowries, Donkeys: The Diary of Niccolò Machiavelli's Father, Messer Bernardo, in Quattrocento Florence* (Frankfurt: Peter Lang, 2002), p. 154.

4. For the manuscript of Lucretius, see Sergio Bertelli, "Noterelle Machiavelliane: Un Codice di Lucrezio e Terenzio," *Rivista Storica Italiana* 73 (1961), pp. 544–53.

5. There is no solid evidence that Machiavelli's opposition to Savonarola, though recognized by his friends, was public knowledge. On these matters, see Nicolai Rubinstein, "The Beginnings of Niccolò Machiavelli's Career in the Florentine Chancellery," *Italian Studies* 11 (1956),

pp. 72–91; and Nicolai Rubinstein, "Machiavelli and the World of Florentine Politics," in *Studies on Machiavelli*, ed. Myron P. Gilmore (Sansoni: Florence, 1972), p. 6.

6. Nicolai Rubinstein, *The Palazzo Vecchio, 1298-1532: Government, Architecture and Imagery in the Civic Palace of the Florentine Republic* (Oxford: Clarendon Press, 1995), p. 50. This fresco of the Wheel of Fortune has long since been destroyed.

CHAPTER 3

1. The supports of this charming story have recently been undermined by Catherine Atkinson, who argues that the episode actually occurred much later, in 1584, and involved another Bernardo Machiavelli, i.e. Niccolò's son, who was confused by biographers with his grandfather: see *Debts, Dowries, Donkeys*, pp. 135–36.

2. *Legazioni e commissarie*, 3 vols., ed. Sergio Bertelli (Milan: Feltrinelli, 1964), vol. 1, p. 70. All further quotations from Machiavelli's diplomatic correspondence will be from this edition.

3. Quoted in Felix Gilbert, *Machiavelli and Guicciardini: Politics and History in Sixteenth-Century Florence* (Princeton: Princeton University Press, 1965), p. 33. It should be noted, in mitigation, that this political system would ultimately serve Florence for more than two hundred years, an indication that it did provide a reasonably stable form of government. The Signori were assisted by other councils whose members served longer terms and, because of staggered elections, overlapped with them. Leonardo Bruni, in *Laudatio Florentinae Urbis*, composed in about 1403, had given high praise to the "diligence" and "competence" of this type of government.

CHAPTER 4

1. *Inferno*, xxvii, lines 37–38. Here and elsewhere in the text I use the edition of *The Divine Comedy* translated by C.H. Sisson (Oxford: Oxford University Press, 1993).

CHAPTER 6

1. *Il Convivio* (*The Banquet*), trans. Richard Lansing (New York: Garland Publishing, 1990), Book IV, chapter xi.

2. *Inferno*, trans. C.H. Sisson, xxvii, line 76.

Notes

CHAPTER 9

1. Machiavelli makes this argument in the *Discourses*, Book I, chapter xxvii.

2. Pico della Mirandola, *Oration on the Dignity of Man*, trans. A. Robert Caponigri (Washington, D.C.: Regnery Publishing, 1956), p. 8.

CHAPTER 10

1. Machiavelli makes these observations in the *Discourses*, Book I, chapter lvi.

CHAPTER 11

1. Quoted in Ludwig Pastor, *History of the Popes*, 40 vols. (London: Kegan Paul, 1891–1953), vol. 6, p. 308.

2. See Michael Rocke, *Forbidden Friendships: Homosexuality and Male Culture in Renaissance Florence* (Oxford: Oxford University Press, 1996).

CHAPTER 12

1. Landucci, *A Florentine Diary*, p. 243.

CHAPTER 14

1. For how Machiavelli's abrasive manner made enemies in Florence and may have contributed to his fall from power, see John M. Najemy, "The Controversy Surrounding Machiavelli's Service to the Republic," in *Machiavelli and Republicanism*, ed. Gisela Bock, Quentin Skinner, and Maurizio Viroli (Cambridge: Cambridge University Press, 1990), pp. 101–17.

2. There has been some confusion whether Niccolò Machiavelli was held in the Stinche or, as most biographers assume, the Bargello. However, a contemporary report clearly states that Machiavelli was confined "in the Stinche." See the remarks of Bartolomeo Cerretani, cited in Oreste Tommasini, *La vita e gli scritti di Niccolò Machiavelli nella loro relazione col machiavellismo*, 2 vols. (Rome: Loescher, 1883–1911), vol. 2, p. 468. The Bargello (known in 1513 as the Palazzo del Podestà) was not used as a prison until after 1574, when the office of *podestà* was abolished by the Medici and the building given to the chief of police. It was certainly the site where prisoners, such as Savonarola, were tortured, but Savonarola was held not in the Palazzo del Podestà but (like Cosimo de' Medici before him) in the *alberghettino*, the "little hotel" in the tower of the Palazzo della Signoria.

3. Quoted in H.C. Butters and J.N. Stephens, "New Light on Machiavelli," *English Historical Review*, vol. 97 (1982), p. 59.

4. The poem has been translated into English by Cecil Grayson in Roberto Ridolfi, *The Life of Niccolò Machiavelli* (Chicago: University of Chicago Press, 1963), p. 137; and by Allan Gilbert, in *Machiavelli: The Chief Works and Others* (Durham, NC: Duke University Press, 1965), vol. 2, p. 1013. My citations are from the Grayson translation.

5. Quoted in Pasquale Villari, *The Life and Times of Girolamo Savonarola*, trans. Linda Villari (London, 1888), p. 308. For Savonarola's torturing, see pp. 299–302.

6. The full translation can be found in Gilbert, *Machiavelli: The Chief Works and Others*, vol. 2, p. 880.

CHAPTER 15
1. A full translation of this famous letter may be found in *Machiavelli and His Friends*, Atkinson and Sices, eds., pp. 262–65.

2. *The Prince*, trans. George Bull (London: Penguin 1999), p. 21. All further quotations from *The Prince* will be from this edition.

3. *The Decameron*, trans. G.H. McWilliam (London: Penguin, 1972), p. 83.

CHAPTER 16
1. *Machiavelli: The Chief Works and Others*, trans. Gilbert, vol. 2, p. 199. All further quotations from the *Discourses* will be from this edition.

CHAPTER 17
1. *Orlando Furioso*, trans. Guido Waldman (Oxford: Oxford University Press, 1983), Canto xxxiii, line 2; Canto xxxvii, line 8.

2. *The Comedies of Machiavelli*, ed. and trans. David Sices and James B. Atkinson (Hanover, N.H.: University Press of New England, 1985), p. 159. All quotations from Machiavelli's comedies will be from this edition.

3. *Life of Castruccio Castracani*, trans. Andrew Brown (London: Hesperus Press, 2003), p. 3.

CHAPTER 18
1. "Ricordi," in Francesco Guicciardini, *Opere*, ed. Vittorio Caprariis (Milan and Naples: Riccardo Riccardi Editore, 1953), p. 120.

2. Ridolfi, *The Life of Niccolò Machiavelli*, p. 291.

CHAPTER 19

1. Giorgio Vasari, "Life of Giovan Francesco Rustico," in *The Lives of the Painters, Sculptors and Architects*, 4 vols., ed. William Gaunt (London: Dent, 1963), vol. 3, p. 33.

CHAPTER 20

1. Johann Georg Walch, ed., *Dr. Martin Luther's Saemmtliche Schriften*, 24 vols. (St. Louis: Concordia Publishing House, n.d.), vol. 18, p. 245.

CONCLUSION

1. Giovan Battista Busini, quoted in Ridolfi, *The Life of Niccolò Machiavelli*, p. 248. Ridolfi is careful to point out that Busini is "a malicious and hostile commentator" (ibid.).

2. Richard Christie, *Studies in Machiavellianism* (St. Louis: Academic Press, 1970).

3. *The Prince* has also been read as a satire by Garrett Mattingly: "Machiavelli's *Prince*: Political Science or Political Satire?" *The American Scholar* 27 (1958), pp. 482–91. For a good discussion of Machiavelli's rehabilitation during the Enlightenment, see Viroli, *Machiavelli* (Oxford: Oxford University Press), p. 115.

4. Mattingly, "Machiavelli's *Prince*"; Vögelin, *History of Political Ideas: Renaissance and Reformation*, eds. David Morse and William Thompson (Columbia, Missouri: University of Missouri Press, 1998); Viroli, *Machiavelli*; J. G. A. Pocock, *The Machiavellian Moment: Florentine Political Thought and the Atlantic Republican Tradition* (Princeton: Princeton Univesity Press, 1975); and Quentin Skinner, *The Foundations of Modern Political Thought*, vol. 1: *The Renaissance* (Cambridge: Cambridge University Press, 1978).

5. Hanna Fenichel Pitkin, *Fortune Is a Woman: Gender and Politics in the Thought of Niccolò Machiavelli* (Berkeley: University of California Press, 1984).

Selected Bibliography

The Comedies of Machiavelli, ed. and trans. James B. Atkinson and David Sices (Hanover, N.H.: University Press of New England, 1985).

Machiavelli and His Friends: Their Personal Correspondence, ed. and trans. James B. Atkinson and David Sices (DeKalb, Ill.: Northern Illinois University Press, 1996).

Machiavelli: The Chief Works and Others, 3 vols., trans. Allan Gilbert, (Durham, N.C.: Duke University Press, 1965).

Machiavelli, Niccolò, *Legazioni e commissarie*, 3 vols., ed. Sergio Bertelli (Milan: Feltrinelli, 1964).

Machiavelli, Niccolò, *The Prince*, trans. George Bull (London: Penguin, 1999).

Ridolfi, Roberto, *The Life of Niccolò Machiavelli*, trans. Cecil Grayson (Chicago: University of Chicago Press, 1963).

Villari, Pasquale, *Niccolò Machiavelli e i suoi tempi illustrati con nuovi documenti*, 3 vols. (Florence: Le Monnier, 1877–82).

EMINENT LIVES

GET A LIFE. BETTER YET, GET ALL OF THEM.

When the greatest writers of our time take on the greatest figures in history, people whose lives and achievements have shaped our view of the world, the resulting narratives—sharp, lively, and original—allow readers to see that world in a whole new way.